Transformed

Transformed

Renewed and

Changed by the

Power of God

CLASSEMINARS, Inc.

WinePressPublishing
Great Books, Defined.

WinePress Publishing (PO Box 428, Enumclaw, WA 98022) functions only as book publisher. As such, the ultimate design, content, editorial accuracy, and views expressed or implied in this work are those of the author.

Transformed cover photo was taken by Sandra Scott, Tucson, Arizona.

Scripture references marked NIV are taken from the *Holy Bible, New International Version®, NIV®*. Copyright © 1973, 1978, 1984 by Biblica, Inc.™ Used by permission of Zondervan. All rights reserved worldwide. www.zondervan.com

Scripture references marked KJV are taken from the *King James Version* of the Bible.

Scripture references marked NASB are taken from the *New American Standard Bible*, © 1960, 1963, 1968, 1971, 1972, 1973, 1975, 1977 by The Lockman Foundation. Used by permission.

Scripture references marked NRSV are taken from the *New Revised Standard Version Bible: Anglicized Edition*, copyright 1989, 1995, Division of Christian Education of the National Council of the Churches of Christ in the United States of America. Used by permission. All rights reserved.

Scripture references marked TNIV are taken from the *Holy Bible, Today's New International Version®*. Copyright © 2001, 2005 by Biblica®. Used by permission of Biblica®. All rights reserved worldwide.

Scripture references marked ESV are taken from *The Holy Bible: English Standard Version*, copyright © 2001, Wheaton: Good News Publishers. Used by permission. All rights reserved.

Scripture references marked TEV are taken from *The Bible in Today's English* (Good News Bible), © American Bible Society 1966, 1971, 1976. Used by permission.

Scripture references marked NLT are taken from the *Holy Bible, New Living Translation*, copyright © 1996, 2004, 2007 by Tyndale House Foundation. Used by permission of Tyndale House Publishers, Inc., Carol Stream, Illinois 60188. All rights reserved.

Scripture marked MSG are taken from *The Message*. Copyright © 1993, 1994, 1995, 1996, 2000, 2001, 2002. Used by permission of NavPress Publishing Group.

ISBN 13: 978-1-4141-2216-8
ISBN 10: 1-4141-2216-0
Library of Congress Catalog Card Number: 2011917657

Welcome to *Transformed.*

We believe the scripture found in Romans 12:2 is life changing. "Do not be conformed to the pattern of this world, but be transformed by the renewing of your mind. Then you will be able to test and approve what God's will is—His good, pleasing, and perfect will."

God is not the God of tweaks; He is the God of transformation. He changes people. My transformation was radical and thorough. What about yours? If you live from your transformation, others will be changed too. Transformation is our message.

You will read about transformed hearts, transformed marriages, transformed students, transformed leaders, transformed physical health, transformed parents and children, and transformed spiritual lives.

So put your feet up, grab a cup of tea, and enjoy the stories of transformed people who have been renewed and changed by the power of God.

We'd love to hear about your transformation too.

Email us at kporterclasseminars@gmail.com

Karen Porter

General Editor

Dedication

CLASSEMINARS, Inc. is pleased to dedicate this book to John Van Diest

John Van Diest, associate publisher at Tyndale House Publishers and founder and former publisher at Multnomah Publishers, has helped bring the world wonderful books.

Van Diest attended Lewis and Clark College, Multnomah University, and Dallas Theological Seminary. He holds degrees in theology and history.

As a publisher, John believes the best books are yet to be published.

He has authored a series of books on *10 Reasons Why* and with Alice Gray and Steve Stephens, he published thirteen titles of *Lists to Live By.*

John is a friend to CLASS and an advocate for Christian Literature. We thank you John for your support and encouragement. We are pleased to dedicate *Transformed* to John Van Diest.

Contents

Special thanks

To the attendees, faculty, and staff of CLASS Christian Writers Conference. May the world be changed and renewed because you told your stories of transformation.

To Gerry Wakeland for your leadership and vision for CLASSEMINARS, Inc. Your commitment to reaching the world for Jesus inspires us all.

To the editorial team of Karen Porter, Linda Gilden, Candy Arrington, Tama Westman, Gloria Penwell, and Lessie Harvey. There are stars in your crowns for your commitment to excellence and your long hours of work.

Sandra Scott

Any Bush Will Do

I STOOD AT my kitchen sink and felt a sudden stillness around me, followed by that familiar voice.

"Take a picture of the bush in your backyard." Protest rose up, but was suppressed.

"Really? The bush in my backyard?" I asked. Hearing it from my own mouth did not make it sound more sensible. The bush was within easy eyeshot, straight out my kitchen window. The branches swayed with the summer breeze. Cutting it back at the proper time birthed yellow and orange blossoms, full and thick. But this plant was common and could be seen on every other corner in my home city. *Take a picture of that old thing?*

My first trip to Maui had been a few weeks before. Vicki, a new Christian friend, and former roommate at the CLASS Christian Writer's Conference, invited me for a visit to her home. I was free to roam, rest, and write for twelve fantastic days. As an amateur photographer, I returned home with hundreds of pictures.

The opportunity arose to enter a photography contest and submit a picture showing transformation. The winner would receive a full tuition for the writer's conference. I was confident. At least one of the Maui photos would make a beautiful entry. I sorted through all the pictures once, then twice; gorgeous seascapes, breathtaking mountain vistas, brilliant exotic plants, lush bamboo forests, and more. To my frustration, not one picture satisfied the submission requirement.

The deadline drew closer. I had no photograph.

The Lord was giving me an exercise in the transformation of my thinking. He invites us not to dig into the same old box of common reasoning and natural habits. We need to be open to the ordinary, willing to listen to His voice and obey.

Transformed

I started snapping pictures of my ever-so-common Mexican Bird of Paradise bush. After about fifty shots with and without backgrounds, He seemed to whisper, "Move higher." In doing so, I exchanged my viewfinder for His. I settled on the one chosen as the cover winner of this book.

God spoke to Moses through an ordinary desert shrub. I imagine Moses saw it in a different light after his experience with the Lord. As a preacher once said, "Any old bush will do." God has the habit of changing what is common into something that is now full of meaning and power. It's not the bush that makes the event unique, but our response to God in obedience. Renewed thinking leads to transformation.

How exciting! God invites us to turn the page to see things in a new way and lives are transformed.

Sandra Scott is an RN, writer, and amateur photographer residing in Tucson, Arizona. She ministers to those seeking healing from the wounds of abortion through Rachel's Vineyard Ministry. Sandra has published devotions and children's short stories. She can be contacted at sandratmc55@yahoo.com.

Eddie Jones

Fake It 'til You Make It

> "Remember your leaders, those who spoke the word of God to you; consider the outcome of their way of life, and imitate their faith."
>
> —Hebrews 13:7 NRSV

IGREW UP on a dirt road with few friends in my neighborhood—any home within bike-riding distance. When I wanted to play basketball, I'd pick two teams (the Lakers and Celtics, for example) and pretend I was the clutch player for both squads. Lobbing the ball to the post, I'd run into position and catch the pass, pivot, and launch a Wilt Chamberlain skyhook. If I missed, Bill Russell would rebound and feed the ball to Jo Jo White who would shoot a jump shot. I kept score in my head, called fouls on myself, and played until Mom called me in for dinner.

Football was more difficult. I'd throw the ball deep and sprint to catch it, sometimes slamming into the pecan tree. Unless it was an obvious pass interference call (occasionally a branch would hold me as I sprinted past), I'd limp back to the huddle and call for a sweeping half-back reverse to allow my wide receivers to rest. The imaginary NFL "Snow Bowl" Championship of '68 played between the Green Bay Packers and Los Angeles Rams remains a classic in my small neighborhood.

I never played organized football or basketball. All the moves I learned came from emulating the legends of the game. But as I grew older and entered college, other players would comment on my abilities, asking if I'd played high school ball. I'd smile, think of Wilt, and launch a skyhook.

These days I study great writers. One day I hope to become one.

Which is why I find it comforting that the writer of Hebrews also endorsed this "fake it 'til you make it" approach to excellence. Imitate the faith of your leaders, he tells his readers, and consider their success. So I do.

I consider the life of David and how his righteous anger for God led him to challenge giants. Stand firm until you are courageous, I tell myself.

I look to Abraham and admire his adventurous spirit and resolute faith as he set out for a land of promise. I think, cling to God's promises regardless of the circumstances.

I'm in awe of Noah and his determination to build a boat miles from the sea. Pray to catch God's vision, I whisper within the depths my darkest doubts.

I can't prove there is a God. Can't prove there isn't either. This is why they call it "faith." But I know this. The grass stains on my knees and the mud splattered on my face, reflected my belief that the game I played on that solitary field behind my mom's house was more real than any I watched on television. I also know the natural inclination of my sinful nature was and still is to be a sorry scoundrel.

And yet, there are moments when I say, act, and love in a way only Christ can. That is nothing less than God "re-making" this faker. Want to be transformed? Ask Christ to captain your team.

"You became imitators of us and of the Lord, … And so you became a model to all the believers in Macedonia and Achaia."

—1 Thessalonians 1:6-7 TNIV

Eddie Jones is co-founder of Christian Devotions Ministry and Acquisition Editor for Lighthouse Publishing of the Carolinas. He is the author of seven nonfiction books, one young adult novel, *The Curse of Captain LaFoote*, and an adult romance, *Bahama Breeze*.

Glenda Durano

Breaking the Rules

USE DASHES, NOT semicolons. Avoid passive voice. Start with dialogue or humor. And for heaven's sake, show—don't tell. I'm learning the rules of writing in order to communicate more clearly with my readers. I don't understand the rules, but I'll do my best to follow them. Just tell me this: What gives some guy in Chicago the right to tell me what I can and can't do in my writing? (Can you tell I haven't learned the rule about not starting a sentence with "and" yet?)

Sure, rules keep things unified and easy to understand. Rules give us a box to put things in (or should I say a box in which to put things?). Sometimes, however, rules cause us to compare things to the norm when, in reality, there is no norm as in the case of transformation.

Experience tells me transformation has to do with dramatic moves of God—hearing His voice, answering the call, and letting God have His way. I think of stories of overwhelming tragedy bringing tears to readers' eyes and glory to God.

But what if I don't have tragedy in my life? Does that mean God hasn't transformed me? I want to follow the "rules of transformation," but I find nothing resembling the norm.

I listen to the stories of those around me. I do not have flashbacks of abuse. I was not miraculously saved from a deadly car accident. I have been married to the same loving man for twenty-five years. My children are nothing short of amazing.

My testimony is plain vanilla. But vanilla isn't so bad, especially when it comes to ice cream—rich and flavorful, leaving you wanting more. Able to accommodate chocolate sauce, caramel coating, strawberries, Oreos®, sprinkles, and a cherry on top—all at the same time! (And before you say anything, I know. This paragraph is full of broken rules, but stay with me. I do it to prove a point.)

As I peruse my past, I see how God has worked Psalm 27 in my life. He has kept me safe and set me high upon a rock. He has hidden me more times than I know. Why has He blessed me and protected me from painful crossroads? I don't know. Does a life of favor mean my life has been shallow and meaningless and I have no testimony? No.

My transformation has been more like squishy, pink Play-doh© in the Master Potter's hands than the slice-and-dice, spectacular transformations that most of my colleagues have experienced. I'm not always putty in God's hands. Not by any means. He's had to pound me and roll me out a few times, but as He shapes me and makes me, He breaks all the rules so I know beyond a shadow of a doubt that He is the Potter, and I am the clay.

Has life been perfect? Not according to me, but who am I to judge? I have learned not to compare my transformation to others. God has taught me He doesn't have to follow any rules.

Am I in denial? Maybe. The "rules of transformation" would say you must have a cause and an effect, black and white. My life, however, is grey, with black and white constantly intermingling, forcing me to follow relationship over rules. Life is transformation—inevitable, intentional, and inexplicable.

Unlike grammar, there are no rules of transformation except the ones we put on ourselves. Certainly I could judge my life, wishing I had a tragedy to tell, but I won't do that. I'm incredibly grateful for God's mercies and grace: a faithful husband, two beautiful daughters, and devoted family and friends. If anything changes, I pray I will still be grateful for His transforming power. Much like passive verbs, a blessed existence may not make for an on-the-edge-of-your-seat writing experience (I think I just made up an adjective. Is that against the rules too?), but it has given me an incredible life.

I'm off to the editor's meeting to see what will be cut and corrected. I'm glad that God is my Editor. And my Author. And I love that He breaks the rules.

An independent education consultant, Glenda Durano helps high school students find colleges that are a great fit. She is the author of *The Christian's Guide to College Admissions* and speaks frequently to students and parents about faith-based college planning. For more information, visit her website at www.collegeadvisingandplanning.com.

Florence Littauer

My Desires Will Be His Desires

SHORTLY AFTER FRED and I became believing Christians and before we had any idea God was much more than a reason to go to church on Sunday, we went to the country club one Saturday evening. The club was the center of our social life, and we always attended the weekend parties and formal dances. This one evening we were sitting at our usual table with our usual friends when I suddenly saw the setting as if for the first time. The conversation seemed pointless and the people pathetic. I realized they had all been drinking too much and weren't even making sense. Since we had always been considered squares because we didn't drink, we had tried to be the life of the party and go along with their behavior no matter what it was. This charade had never bothered me because I wanted so much to be an accepted part of the club elite.

I can picture that evening with Fred looking movie-star handsome in his tuxedo and me in one of my many gowns. The man next to me, whom I knew well, had his arm around me and was noisily kissing my shoulder. Suddenly he looked pitiful, and I had an urge to push him off his chair. I glanced across at Fred, and a voluptuous, tipsy woman was hanging on him and batting her false eyelashes up and down his face. These flirting actions were probably the same that night as they had been many times before, but I saw them with new eyes. I had no idea why things looked different to me at that time, but as I listened to the same music and stared at the same walls, I wanted to run. I asked myself, *What in the world are we doing here?*

In the car going home I sighed to Fred, "Do you know what thought went through my head tonight?"

Before I got any further he added, "Let me guess because it might be the same as mine. I looked around at the people and the place and asked myself, 'What in the world are we doing here?'"

I screamed in excitement over our identical thoughts, and if the angel Gabriel had suddenly appeared on the hood of our car, we couldn't have been more spiritually moved. God had spoken to us both at the same time with the same message. On the way home we agreed not to return to the club, and we never went back again. God didn't forbid us from going there and He didn't burn the club down; He just changed our desires.

God is faithful to meet us where we are in our lives. Once we receive Christ in our hearts, as Savior, the Holy Spirit begins to teach us how to make Him Lord of every area of our lives. As we become intimate with Him, His desires will become our desires.

Florence Littauer is known around the world as a woman of encouraging words. The author of more than 30 books, Florence is founder of CLASSEMINARS, Inc. This story is an excerpt from *The Gift of Encouraging Words*, Word Publishing, 1995.

Melissa Keller

Eternal Eyes

I BELIEVE ALL of those who unashamedly claim Jesus Christ as Lord live in a state of constant change, an ever-progressing transformation toward becoming more like the King. For when we bear the blood mark of a race redeemed, how then can we live otherwise? But at times there are moments that stand above the rest, painfully beautiful life lessons that demand to be shared. These milestones along the earthly road are not meant to be held within, secret and safe from all eyes but our own. These revelations and moments of brazen grace are tales on the pages of our earthly existence, words that touch the tongues of poets and yet still are nothing but unworthy description.

With our mouths and hands, we offer our human praise, though only shadows in a dim reflection. The Story of Love transcends the skill of man's pen. Even so, I offer my thoughts in response to a dare, a challenge to name 1,000 blessings I have been given, both great and small. In choosing to see beyond the confines of life's pain, we find ourselves filled with thankfulness and suddenly surprised by joy.

In the loneliest of moments,
In the silence of empty space,
In the stillness of a whisper,
We may hear the voice of grace.
The tongue that quiets fears,
And whispers I Am God,
The ear that hears and knows the pain,
Of the earthly land we trod.
And when tears of strife flowed free,
Upon my knees I cried,

Transformed

Father, I have seen this world,
For this, oh God, you died?
I claimed your faithful promise,
To always be near my soul,
But still I stood in darkness,
On the edge of emptiness whole.
Your word I had long searched,
And then at last upon my knees,
I asked you where to find this joy,
I begged you, Father, please.
No words could I discern then,
No holy prophet's creed,
But within the pages of a friend,
I was offered a tiny seed.
This little humbling grain of truth,
Transformed into a dare,
A dare to live a thankful life,
To name my gifts with care.
With Adam's mouth I called them out,
The list of blessings mine,
And voiced them into being,
These gifts in holy rhyme.
I filled my hands with broken earth,
In pain, lifted them high,
For here within created earth,
I was given the land and sky.
For eyes that choose to openly see,
Still feel the pain of life,
But in daring to pursue the beautiful,
We may rise above our strife.
When mornings of woe dawn for me.
I choose to see instead,
The liquid gold of the rising sun,
As oil upon my head.
When darkness closes round,
The cursèd black of night,
I sing of frozen diamond stars,
And the milk-glow of moonlight.

Eternal Eyes

In moments of brilliant beauty,
When I dance with glory's son,
I bring my praise to the ancient gates,
And thank El Elyon.
When the pain stabs long and deep,
My bleeding feet I bare,
And thank my God for His great love,
On holy ground I dare.
Upon the bier of sacrifice,
I burn my selfish pride,
I drink from wineskins given anew,
And I cast the old aside.
For eyes that choose to see,
What oft they had long missed,
See passion in the suffering heart,
And the touch of a holy kiss.
When the storms of life take hold,
When hearts are gripped with fear,
We clench our hands in vain control,
And lose sight of blessings near.
But the eternal and earthly gaze,
Can pierce the darkening veil,
Voice giving essence to simple grace,
Can steady a hope that fails.
The cup of life I take and hold,
My lips sing of His praise,
And so it shall be evermore,
Unto the ending of my days.
The love song of the ages,
Is the blood of my rescued soul,
I give thanks for o'er 1000 gifts,
And see as He makes me whole.

Inspired by J.R.R. Tolkien and C.S. Lewis, Melissa Keller has written purposeful prose ever since her first notebook. In her spare time, Melissa rides horses, dances, plays guitar, and revels in the beauty of creation. Neighborhood children light up her eyes and she enjoys leading them on horse rides.

John Van Diest

Where There is Smoke, There is Fire

IT MIGHT BE a small transformation in the eyes of an adult, but for a ten-year-old boy it was huge.

We were a family of five, Dad, Mom, older brother Gale, older sister Fae, and me. We lived in a small rural area near Sedro Wooley, Washington, called by the Indian name the Skagic River Valley. As The Depression ruled most of our survival decisions, my parents became expert dairy farmers. The farm provided the essentials for survival. While most of my childhood memories of play, school, animals, and hunting reflect the challenges of being quite poor, an understanding of the Bible, God, and salvation are absent. Looking back, I now realize why. Dad and Mom were running from a somewhat rigid and legalistic religious upbringing. Going to church was last on their list, but spiritual roots began to sprout.

During those early years of The Depression, the pastor of the small local church also drove the school bus to make ends meet. He had regular contact with my parents, who respected him as bus driver, but intentionally avoided any scent of his beliefs, particularly if they were connected to the church.

Dad was tough, a man of few words, and a strong disciplinarian. It was not unusual for us (mostly me) to receive weekly spankings with his belt or some other nearby punishing rod. In today's law he might be charged with child abuse.

Dad was a chain-smoker. Like many in those days, he rolled his own cigarettes. Almost all of our male relatives were smokers. In my memory, all men smoked, except the preacher. The smoke of the day was cigarettes, with a cigar for special occasions.

While we kids were forbidden to smoke, we found ways to smoke secretly. Sometimes, it was cigarettes. Other times, we smoked a unique piece of perforated wood.

Where There is Smoke, There is Fire

When I was about ten years old, our uneventful lives were invaded by God. That's when, through a mostly silent witness, our local pastor led my parents to faith in Christ, and as a result, the whole family professed Christ.

Dad felt the need, prompted by the Holy Spirit, to stop smoking. He tried and tried but just couldn't kick the habit. Stopping smoking became the first real test of his new-found faith. Dad and Mom prayed, and his new Christian friends prayed. Even the preacher prayed publicly in church that God would release him from his dirty habit, to no avail.

One day his lips began to swell any time he lit up. After weeks of off-and-on struggle with the sore mouth, the issue boiled down to either stop smoking or live with swollen lips. God won. Dad stopped smoking.

As a child of ten, I was also a new believer. I watched my dad's relatively small habit become a major one. Then, I witnessed his victory over his smoking habit. I saw first-hand God's power and the power of prayer in transforming a chain smoker to a non-smoker.

A champion of Christian publishing throughout the world, John Van Diest is an Associate Publisher at Tyndale House Publishers. Besides being the founding publisher of Multnomah and Vision House publishers, John has a dozen books credited to his authorship and his newest one from Guideposts is *Unsolved Miracles*, volume 2. For more information, contact John at jvandst@aol.com.

Discovering the One Thing

Jerome Daley

G OD HAS BROKEN into my world in several unforgettable moments. The story I'll relate to you now is about one of those moments; it was the awakening of my "one thing." I was thirteen. Eighth grade. I had grown up wanting to know and love God to the best of my ability, but it felt harder now. Some of my friends were making choices I knew would take them away from God, not toward Him. Drinking, smoking, listening to questionable music – not exactly hard-core evil, but the fork in the path was obvious. I stopped, unsure. What would that path hold? How could I continue the path I was on without knowing where other paths would lead?

Then I had a sleepover with one of my junior high buddies and together with a third friend, we lived it up, thirteen-year-old style. I tried my first swallow of whiskey—and was that ever an unpleasant surprise! But still very cool, of course. By the middle of the night, my soul—and my head—were reeling in a cloud of cigarette smoke and vertigo from hours of late-night TV. Were we having fun yet?

Then something deep inside me cried out, *This is not what I was made for! Dad, please come take me home!* The thought of actually calling home crossed my mind. *No, can't do that; definitely uncool.* So I gutted it out until the next morning when Dad did come to pick me up in our old Ford sedan, roughly the size of a Third World country. By that time, the inner crisis had passed in its intensity, and I was feeling a bit numb as we drove through the neighborhood.

"How was your time with the guys?" I'm sure Dad asked.

"Fine," I'm sure I replied.

Then he said something I'll never forget. "You know, a strange thing happened to me last night," Dad said casually. "I woke up in the middle of the night, and it was almost like I could hear you calling me."

Well, that did it! Between the gushing sobs, I managed to get out my story. Dad listened compassionately. I don't remember anything else he actually said, but I will always remember

14

that night. I think of it as the night God called my name. It may have been my dad God woke up, but it was me He was calling. And I heard Him loud and clear. The peace and contentment that flooded my soul were like nothing I had ever known. *He cares about me! A very big God really likes me a lot to go to all the trouble of waking up my dad because I was hurting!*

I knew on that late-spring day of 1979 I had my "one thing" to live for. And that has never changed.

This story is an excerpt from *Soul Space* by Jerome Daley, Integrity Publishers, 2003. Reprinted by permission. "Soul Space: Where God Beaks In," Jerome Daley, copyright 2003, Thomas Nelson Inc. Nashville, Tennessee. All rights reserved.

Jerome Daley is a leadership coach, speaker, and consultant, partnering with strategic leaders and organizations to cultivate a sustainable, healthy inner life. Author of six books, he invites you to examine the assumptions of your daily life. Jerome, his wife, three teenagers, and Malamute make their home in Greensboro, North Carolina. www.purposecoach.net

Linda Marcia

Daily Bread

THE FRONT DOOR burst open and banged against the entry wall.
"Mom, do you want bread?

"What?"

Out of breath, Nick asked me again, "Mom, do you want bread?"

"Okay, I guess." Before I finished the sentence, he waved his arms, signaling someone to come in. Neighborhood kids ran into my house carrying armloads of bread. Laughing and giggling, one by one they dropped familiar loaves and rolls of plastic wrapped bread and ran out for more. Surprised, I stared at a four-foot-high pile of various types of bread on my kitchen floor. I had no idea where this bread came from.

"Stop! You have to stop. That's enough. Nick, tell the kids, no more."

My daughters ran in the house to see what was going on. "Where did all this bread come from?" Nicole asked.

"I don't know. Where did your brother go?"

Nick ran back in.

"Mom, Mom, are you happy? Are you?"

"Where did you get the bread?"

"There's a guy up the street with a bread truck. He asked if anybody wanted his leftover bread. I told him you did, so the kids carried it down the street to our house."

The appearance of that much bread was unusual, but what happened before made it more amazing. My children were home from school and outside playing. I sat on the old couch talking to God, feeling discouraged.

A year after my divorce, I was overwhelmed, responsible for meeting all the needs of my young children. *Where was God?* I wondered if things would ever get better? My business was barely surviving. Many days I struggled to buy groceries to feed a family of four.

Daily Bread

"God, I feel like You have forsaken me. I work hard Lord, but the food is running short. I know Your Word says You will give us our daily bread, but I don't see it."

I had barely finished my sentence when my son blasted through the front door. Now, I had white bread, French bread, wheat bread, rolls, hamburger buns, and hot dog buns. I had bread in the refrigerator and on top of the refrigerator. I had bread in the freezer, bread in the refrigerator in the garage, in the pantry, on all the counters. We gave bread to the neighbors. I gave bread to my friends. That night after the kids were in bed, I marveled at the goodness of God. "Yes Lord, thank You for the bread, but did you have to take me so literally?"

Twenty years later, this experience still fills me with wonder at the extent the Lord will go to teach us about His faithfulness. I remember God's provision and abundance at a time when my faith waned with the heaviness of responsibility. The Lord prepared me for the future. Daily, He is transforming me from an abused wife and mother toward a strong woman of faith.

I didn't know my family would face homelessness, a prodigal child, drug addictions, rehab, and mental illnesses. God was growing my faith so I could endure, so I could believe in the power of His healing grace and provision.

The bread at communion symbolizes His body given for our sins and for our healing. He gives us everything we need for this day and is transforming us for the next. Thank you, Lord, for giving us our daily bread.

Linda Marcia is the mother of three adult children. She enjoys being part of the mission ministry at her church and counsels single women and victims of domestic violence. She owns Decorative Designs, an interior design firm in Capistrano Beach, California, where she resides.

Chad Spriggs

The Whisper

IN THE DARK and aimless space, an overwhelming endless race stretches me beyond repair.

A gentle whisper shouts endless truths throughout, echoing, "Come, draw near."

Yet the fight remains, crippling fatigue and pain, deafening the battle's aim.

A dim shaft of light, casting my shadow's plight, reveals the staggering shame.

I am but a man—tattered, defaced, and torn, unable to keep the pace.

Deprived of hope, emptied of words I choke, devoid of any case.

Every attempt to run increasingly left undone, nothing left to do.

I await my end, knowing it comes and then, I'm reminded of what is true.

Out of the faint clear, a gentle whisper I hear, "Come, draw near."

It crowds my thoughts and calms my pace, helping me to see;

That all the while I placed myself in torment over me.

Now my steps, pure and swift, come with such ease,

I listen for the whisperer's voice

And quietly release.

The Whisper

"Let us run with endurance the race that is set before us, looking to Jesus,
the founder and perfecter of our faith."

—Hebrews 12:1-2 ESV

Chad Spriggs has become a seasoned pastor with a heart that longs to reach, teach, search, and move people toward a deeper love for God. Chad's desire to teach God's truth, grow biblical community, and create compelling music guides him to become more like Christ. Visit www.chadspriggs.com for more information.

Larry J. Leech II

Robots

THE ELDERLY MAN sat in his rocker watching his only grandson. His heart ached for the boy, hoping he kept a sweet, gentle spirit instead of growing into an angry young man.

"Vroom. Vroom." The child pushed the toy car across the hardwood floor of the living room. Around chair legs, over the rug. He crawled, curving the car right and left, hairpin turns that, in real life, would not be possible.

"You racing?"

The boy's brow furrowed. "I'm driving fast, Grandpa. Running from bad guys."

Running, the old man thought, remembering his younger days when he sped away from problems: a fight with his mother over not cleaning his room; a heated exchange with his brother over a pair of socks, from a restaurant after arguing with a waiter.

He hung his head. Speeding away. Always away. As fast as he could. And when he couldn't speed away, he'd made life miserable for those around him.

"Why are you so moody?" a co-worker once asked.

Without hesitating, he answered. "I guess so I can dictate how everyone acts around me. If I want fun, I'm in a good mood. If I don't want to be bothered, I'm in a bad mood."

The co-worker had shaken her head and gone back to work.

"Watch this, Grandpa."

He shifted in his chair. "Careful now. Grandma'll get us both if we break something."

The chase continued, complete with engine revving, tires squealing. Finally, the eight-year-old lay on his stomach and flipped over the car. He pulled on the tires and twisted the frame.

"Stop that," the grandfather ordered.

Robots

The boy twisted a few more parts, snapped them into a new position, and held up the finished product. "Look, a robot," he said with a gap-toothed grin. "He's bigger and stronger than when he's a car."

"Let me see." The grandfather slid out of his rocker, reaching for the transformed car. He examined the toy, rotating it back and forth in his hands. "Make it a car again," he said, handing it back.

Seconds later the boy gave back the toy, now in its original shape of a yellow and black Camaro.

"Interesting," the old man mumbled as he accepted the toy. He rolled it back and forth on the floor. The wheels worked fine. He made tight turns and caught himself making the same car noises his grandson had.

"I'm going to get another toy. You can play with that one," the boy said as he ran from the room.

More running, the man thought, again mourning the decades he'd spent running from those who loved him.

Until.

The night he'd driven away from the love of his life, the night he almost lost her. After another heated argument about something that happened long before he entered the picture, he fled. Ran as he always had.

He drove long into the night. But the farther away from home he got, the farther away from her he traveled, the worse he felt. This woman meant too much. He needed to change, or he'd spend the rest of his life alone. Desperate, he prayed, asking God to change him.

The change took time. One day, one moment at a time. He attended an anger management seminar. With each small victory, he became stronger, and his anger and hatred of others began to fade. Needing something tangible, he placed a note in front of the computer monitor on his office desk: *Love my people.*

If he hadn't begun learning when he had, he wouldn't be here now, with this wonderful child, whom he loved with all his heart.

The boy returned; the grandfather passed the car back to him. "Make it a robot again."

His grandson took the car, twisted and pulled. Then offered it like a gift. "Here you go."

The grandfather took the robot and studied it through teary eyes.

"What's wrong, Grandpa?"

"Nothing." The elderly man wiped his eyes with the back of his hand. "I'm fine."

The grandfather eased back into his rocker. He held the robot with both hands, thankful he himself didn't have to change back into his former self. Speeding away from problems and driving away loved ones was no way to live.

"Want me to make it a car again, Grandpa?"

He smiled at his grandson. "No, buddy. I think he likes being a robot just fine."

Larry J. Leech II is a ghostwriter, editor, and Executive Chairman of Christian Writers Guild Word Weavers. He and his wife Wendy live in Central Florida, and their son Chris lives in the New England area.

Marilyn Neuber Larson

But I Didn't Win

WITH HAMMERING HEART and Jell-O© knees, I walked to the podium for the district Toastmistress International speech contest.

Why am I scared? Is it because I want to win, or because I'm afraid to face the future alone after my recent divorce?

My first word escaped in a squeak, which shook my confidence. I glanced at the audience and saw an elderly man's chin resting on his chest. When he snored, I lost my place. His wife nudged him, and he jerked awake. I hoped he wasn't a judge.

When the other two speakers concluded, the contest timer announced, "Two contestants are disqualified because they ran overtime. Only the remaining contestant qualifies." Then he announced my name.

Afterwards, a smiling woman shook my hand. I immediately liked her.

"Hi," she said, "I just wanted to meet you. I won the speech contest for my district. We'll be competing against each other at the next level."

"It's embarrassing to win by default," I said. "The other two speeches were terrific."

The second speech contest was impromptu, but we were given ten-minutes to prepare. Time ran out before my ending jelled and my sketchy outline terrified me. My speech was a stone-cold, serious, disappointing talk.

When Jane, my new friend and witty opponent, stepped to the podium she began her story with humor. The laughter was a welcome relief.

I was presented second place—out of two. I congratulated Jane. "Your speech was great. What a relief. I won't have to speak at the next level."

Three weeks later Jane called. "I have an emergency and can't attend the speech contest. Will you go to Tucson in my place?"

"I couldn't do it justice," I admitted. "I only won by default, and the contest falls on the last day of school."

Jane said, "Let's pray about it."

We hung up the phone, and I prayed, "Lord, You know I didn't win. Do You want me to go to this contest? How can I get a talk ready in time? They need my answer tomorrow."

The next morning, I found my devotional book buried under layers of papers. I got a cup of coffee and opened the book. "Here I am five days behind," I said to God. "Who wants to read Exodus on Monday morning? I'd rather read Philippians."

Read Exodus, I felt God say.

When I found the passage, these words jumped off the page of my *Good News Bible:* "But Moses said, 'No Lord, don't send me. I have never been a good speaker, and I haven't become one since you began to speak to me. I am a poor speaker, slow and hesitant.' The Lord said to him, 'Who gives man his mouth? Who makes him deaf or dumb? Who gives him sight or makes him blind? It is I, the Lord. Now, go! I will help you to speak, and I will tell you what to say'" (Exodus 4:10-12 TEV).

Almighty God, Creator of the Universe, spoke directly to me while I was sitting there in my nightgown. Amazing!

Holy God gave me His specific answer: "Now go!" And it came with His promise: "I will help you speak, and I will tell you what to say." How could I argue with God? There was nothing to do except call Jane and accept.

Suddenly, I no longer felt alone. My life had changed. God answered my prayer, and He gave me a promise directly from Scripture. That was the beginning of a deepening relationship. I experienced His overwhelming love, and realized if He answered once, He would do it again.

That morning in the margin of my Bible I wrote the following notation. "God, do you want me to go to the Tucson speech contest? How can I get my talk ready in time?" I added the date and highlighted His remarkable answer.

Since then, I've talked to God in prayer, and He often replies to me with Scripture. Sometimes, when I look through old Bibles I read the margins, and read my life.

Although I didn't win a prize in Tucson, I took away new-found confidence. I was no longer afraid because I was not alone. God helped me speak, and He told me what to say.

Marilyn Neuber Larson is an author and speaker who lives in Albuquerque, New Mexico. She married Bill, her farmer hero, and became Pumpkin Queen after she retired from teaching school. She continues to ask God questions, and her Bibles are filled with the notes and dated, highlighted passages of His awesome answers.

Steve McCoy

The Round Pen

JOHN, AN OLD cowboy who hobbled more than he walked, entered the arena while several thousand of us watched. A bow legged, good ol' boy cowboy, with his hands in his pockets and the "aw shucks" attitude that fit well into his jeans, flannel shirt, and wide brim hat personality. Today he planned to show us how to deal with an unbroken horse, saddling it and riding within a two-hour span. Having little experience with horses, I thought his goal more than a little optimistic.

He explained that horses have no natural defense against threats; they have no claws or sharp teeth. Their only defense is to run. Anyone or anything that looks at their hindquarters is a threat.

And so they run.

John said a round pen offers no corners for the horse to hide as he hobbled over to a young horse in the corner of the arena and led it into the round pen. The horse pulled against the lead rope a number of times. How convenient for John as he stood in the middle of the round pen, a coiled rope in one hand, and watched the nervous horse while it ran in circles.

Desperate to get away from John, the horse ran. There was nowhere to go. No corners and no escape from the pen. John was trying to earn the horse's trust by teaching it to turn toward its fear. John waited until the horse would, ever so slightly, turn its head toward him and then he released the pressure and the horse stopped running. After a few minutes of applying and releasing pressure the horse turned fully toward and faced John, now looking to him for direction. Then John turned to us, reminding us of how nervous the applause made the horse earlier and with his back to the horse, he asked us to applaud one more time. This time the horse ran to John for protection.

The horse now trusted John.

God is like this trainer. He will put us in a round pen watching us run in circles, waiting for us to turn our gaze to Him. The woman caught in adultery (John 8:1-11) was in a round pen. She had been dragged from her bed, and, I suspect, was ill prepared to stand in front of the angry religious people with nothing much but shame to accompany her. It's curious to me that the properly dressed and dignified men knew where to find her. Now she was used for their religious pleasure.

I doubt she lifted her eyes to face them. I envision a circle of "proper" men, rocks in their hands, looking at Jesus as she lay in the dirt, desperate to be anywhere but there.

She was in a round pen.

Nowhere to go. Nowhere to hide. Running in circles.

Jesus bent to write in the dirt. He dealt easily enough with the religious. But He waited for her to turn ever so slightly to Him.

Patience is at the heart of what Jesus does. He gets us in a round pen and lets us run until we are willing to turn and look at Him. I run to find what I think will make me happy, what I think will help me find life. I run because I am afraid. And so I run, and run, and run.

All the while Jesus watches, waiting until I am willing to give Him an ear, to ever so slightly turn my head in His direction. Then, He turns and lets me rest, satisfied I am beginning to look to Him for life and to venture out of my hiding places. And I begin to know His delight.

I am *so* tired of running in circles.

Steve McCoy is an ordinary guy stumbling toward grace while trying to be a husband, father, grandfather, and a dependable man. Growing up in small church and serving in nearly every volunteer position, he forged his faith in the round pen of life. Adapted from the book *What's Love Got to Do With It?*

Emily Easley

Gifts Are Meant To Be Returned

ABANDONING MY DAUGHTER and husband were not part of my weekend plans, but time had come to let them go.

Nausea hit me like a ton of bricks. My body responded to my spirit. Sick to the core. Tears streaming I pleaded, "God, I want to say yes. But nothing is more important to me than Josh and Lillie."

"Exactly, my child," He whispered.

Fear of losing my child smothered me yet again. Before going to this conference, I had met terror face to face in a bookstore. The words of *One Thousand Gifts* written by Ann Voskamp ripped me to the core. Her vivid account of her young sister's tragic accident caused panic to blanket me like darkness of the night. Reading a few pages, I closed the book and put it back on the shelf. I determined this would *not* be a book on my must-read list. Refusing to trust God with Lillie's life, I walked away—leaving Him on the shelf as well.

Months later the same woman whose written words stirred up fear in my soul stood before me in flesh and blood. Her soft-spoken words settled deep within my soul. She spoke about the importance of being thankful in all things, seeing everything as a gift from God, and being willing to live with open hands, releasing gifts back to God when necessary. She challenged us to think of three gifts we thanked God for and one gift we needed to return to Him. She told us to lay the gifts at the foot of the large wooden cross to the right of the stage.

Panic set in. All the small steps of saying yes to God over the past several months led up to this extraordinary step of faith. Immediately I knew God asked me to say yes to Him in a big way.

After writing my gifts on the small card provided, I prepared to join the other ladies. My soul ached. I sensed God's nudge, "No, I want Lillie and Josh. Sit down and mark out the generic gifts. Be specific, give me Lillie and Josh." At that moment, the other women faded. The only two who mattered were God and me. Tears flooded my vision as I struggled to hold on to the two most precious gifts God had given me.

Fighting no longer, I crossed through my generic gifts of fear, doubt, and worry. I wrote, "Josh and Lillie." As if God couldn't sense my heart's desperate cries, I wrote a prayer acknowledging by holding on to them I interfered with God's plan. He could do his greatest work if I didn't try to control life's circumstances. I held them captive in my tight grip.

As I joined the line of women making their journey to the cross, agony consumed me. I was sobbing and physically sick. My heart ached as I looked at their names. Lillie and Josh. This was it. All I had left to offer.

Looking at the cross before me in distress I wondered, "Where should I lay them?" I chose to position them as close to the foot of the cross as possible, leaving no chance of their being alone at any moment between my heart and God's. They were out of my grip and in the arms of their Savior where they belonged.

Reality sank in. I had abandoned my two-year-old, alone with no protection. The intensity was more than I could bear. I struggled not to wail and cry out to Jesus. But in my soul I heard, "Emily, I'm with you. Trust Me. Just trust Me." His tender words assured me I had not abandoned either of them, but provided them the greatest Protector possible. The weight of control lifted as each tear fell.

And then a gift – the embrace of a friend became the arm of God reaching to comfort me.

Releasing Josh and Lillie allowed me to be empty of everything. Empty so God could fill me with the gift of Himself.

Emily Easley has never experienced a shortage of words. However, God is teaching her to distinguish between simply talking versus sharing something of value. Her heart's desire is to serve and glorify God. She's a western Kentucky native, married to her high-school sweetheart and mother to a vivacious, beautiful daughter.

I'm Home

Karen Jordan

A S I WALKED up the sidewalk to Mother's door, I heard loud wails and sobbing. I recognized Mother's voice, so I opened the door and rushed in without knocking. Mother sat on the edge of her rocking chair with her hands covering her face. My sister, Cathy, sat close to Mother on a stool—tissues in hand—ready to provide whatever comfort she would accept. Cathy frowned and shrugged her shoulders as our eyes met.

"Mother, I'm home!" I hurried across the room and embraced her.

"She's been like this all day," Cathy explained as she fought back tears.

Mother's fight with a rare disease caused confusion and darkness to rule her thoughts as she fought an illness destroying her mind. I knelt to hug her. She melted into my arms.

"Mother, are you afraid of dying?" I felt her fear surrounding us.

"No. Of living!"

Mother had faced death before and survived. A few years earlier, when her heart failed during surgery, Mother caught a glimpse of the afterlife. But the darkness terrified her, as she faced the emptiness of her faith. After this horrific experience, Mother sought answers to her questions and fear of dying. And she discovered the missing link in her spiritual life—an intimate relationship with Jesus Christ.

As Mother faced her terminal illness, fear and doubts flooded her. Would Jesus provide an answer to alleviate her fear this time? Could she really trust Him to be with her as she walked through the valley of her impending death?

I couldn't save Mother from the rare disease, but I could choose to trust the Lord to walk through this time with all of us. God reminded me of His promise: "Even though I walk through the darkest valley, I will fear no evil, for you are with me; your rod and your staff, they comfort me" (Psalm 23:4 NLT).

I also recalled His faithfulness through the years. "I was young and now I am old, yet I have never seen the righteous forsaken" (Psalm 37:23 TNIV).

As we walked though Mother's last days, God once again provided all we needed, day by day. Sitting near my mother one day near the end of her journey, I noticed her eyes fixed on the high ceiling in her townhouse living room.

"What do you see, Mother?"

"Heaven," she responded without changing her expression.

Shocked by her answer, I asked, "What does it look like?"

"Huge," she sighed.

What a perfect description of heaven, I thought.

During the next few weeks, Mother lost her ability to communicate. As the end drew near, we sang songs about heaven to Mother and read Scripture.

Although Mother remained silent after sharing her vision of heaven with me, I knew she was convinced it was her destination. And a few weeks later, in the final moment of her life, Mother whispered, "I'm home."

Karen Barnes Jordan is best known for telling the stories that matter most. She has multiple writing credits and trains other writers as well. Contact her for speaking events, writing assignments, and interviews at kj@karenjordan.net or visit www.karenjordan.net.

Jan Johnson

Guilt Doesn't Change You—and It Can Make You Worse

HOW DO PEOPLE change? Sometimes we think that all it takes is feeling bad enough about something—then we'll change. If the guilt is deep enough about what I've done or how I've treated people, then I'm motivated to be different. In other words: Guilt makes you good.

I don't think so. In fact, for the last ten years or so, I've had suspicions that guilt is not helpful at all. When I do something that seems good because I'll feel guilty if I don't do it, then I do it with the wrong heart. Then my attitude shows—people can tell I'm reluctant, not whole-hearted. They're not blessed. I've found this lack of wholeheartedness is corrosive to my life with God.

And for change to occur, we need a "next step." But guilt doesn't help you know what's good, just what's bad. Focusing on what *not* to do makes things worse. If I tell you not to think about pink elephants, your mind will become quite creative in imagining them.

Relief from guilt comes through compunction. I like that old-fashioned, funny-sounding word that can also mean guilt but it's very different. It's more relational toward God and much closer to repentance. When I feel compunction, I don't feel like a jerk but I feel much loved by God. I run to God and say, "What a dumb thing I did! And You are so good to me. Please forgive me." After pausing to receive that forgiveness, I ask God for a next step.

So compunction works well because it sends us to the arms of Jesus to confess. Guilt just makes us hate life. Because compunction sends us into the arms of Jesus, it pinches at first but overall it feels good. It feels clean. We feel relieved and released.

So it's with interest that I recently read an observation that when saints like Ignatius of Loyola and Francis of Assisi and Amy Carmichael felt unholy (because of their sin) in light of God's goodness, they didn't feel depressed and guilt-ridden about it. It didn't make them hate life and not want to think about God. They didn't feel that God gloated over them or felt exasperated with how dumb they were. Instead they focused on God's power to change them and sensed God's empowerment. They felt courageous enough to pick themselves up and cooperate with God in being changed.

Ignatius talks about the effects of guilt on two different kinds of people. As an experienced man of the world who found Christ, he said this:

• If your life is headed away from God and toward doing only what you want, guilt will be helpful to you because it will point you to God. Whatever delights you will probably point you away from God.

• But when our life has begun heading toward God—we really want God for God's own self and we've begun to live in tune with God's intentions for the world—guilt prevents us from moving forward. The self-absorption of guilt distracts us and leads us away from God and into self-obsession. So guilt isn't helpful. When we're headed toward God, what helps is to recognize God's action in our life through how God encourages us and gives us strength and peace (even through tears—but good ones—at times).

The constant spiritual naval gazing that comes with guilt *seems* spiritual, but it's not. It doesn't draw us toward God but further into self-absorption: continual thoughts of me, myself, and I.

So if we're on a path to know God, we ask ourselves: What is God drawing me toward today? Where is God delighting me and inviting me into adventure? Growing sensitive to the drawing of God is transforming (not guilt). Pedro Arrupe put it best:

Nothing is more practical than finding God, than falling in love in a quite absolute, final way. What you are in love with, what seizes your imagination, will affect everything.
It will decide what will get you out of bed in the morning, what you will do with your evening, how you spend your weekends, what you read, whom you know, what breaks your heart, and what amazes you with joy and gratitude. Fall in love, stay in love, and it will decide everything.

Jan Johnson is a writer, speaker, and spiritual director who holds degrees in Christian education and spirituality. She has written seventeen books, including *Enjoying the Presence of God, When the Soul Listens, Savoring God's Word,* and many magazine articles. Jan is a frequent retreat and conference speaker. This story is adapted from September 2010 Wisbit from website of Jan Johnson: www.JanJohnson.org ©Jan Johnson

Taprina Milburn

Renegade Mom

I WATCHED A young mother wrestle with her renegade toddler in a grocery store. The toddler wanted what he wanted and wouldn't have it any other way. She pried a candy bar out of his hands as he kicked and screamed on the floor. Then she led him out the automatic doors crying the whole way.

Some days I feel like that toddler—fists clenched, clinging to a role and time of life I'm not ready to relinquish. But I am a woman who is experiencing a transformation—on my way to becoming a mother of young adults and shedding the responsibilities of caring for the many details of other people's lives. Although I haven't lost a child, I am sensing some grief as one season of my life fades away to make room for the next. I'm uneasy because I don't know what "next" looks like. On some days this new phase feels like ill-fitting hand-me-downs.

We've recently sent our oldest child, Aubrey, to college, and I've caught myself several times setting the table for four, when only three plates are needed. Or I stand at the foot of the stairs and call out her name to come for dinner. Our youngest, Brenner, just turned 16 and drives himself to and from school and church activities. My natural reflex is to reach for my keys when it's time for him to go, only to have him remind me, "Mom, I can drive myself." The door has closed on those conversations we had while I was behind the driver's wheel.

But I don't want to miss out on the opportunity for transformation because I am sitting in the middle of my living room floor sobbing over my kids' baby pictures or filling my newfound free time with "The Housewives of New Jersey" (I've done both). I've known women who have reached this phase of life and instead of seeing it as a growth opportunity have spent years wading through a general feeling of discontent, unsure of what to do without children. Between the baby picture meltdown and "The Housewives" episodes, if I don't embrace this transformation, I will join their ranks.

Transformed

My petitions lately have been, "Lord, walk me through this phase, help me let go of my former role. Show me the satisfaction of what comes next from you, and protect me from not believing you have plans for my future."

As a Christian, the end result of any transformation point in my life—whether it was my salvation experience as a teen or my current mid-life malaise—is to live out God's will. Romans 12:2 tells me I can only see His will if I renew my mind. For me, renewing means placing into His hands the fading role I am clinging to like a renegade toddler.

Comfort comes for me also in knowing through this transformation His Word promises in Jeremiah 29:11, "'For I know the plans I have for you,' declares the Lord, 'plans to prosper you and not to harm you, plans to give you hope and a future.'"

God does not intend for us to wander aimlessly through the empty rooms of our homes or long for roles we once held. I can't see what comes next in my life but I have faith that it will have meaning and direction. My part is to unclench my fists, anticipate how He will fill the empty rooms of my heart with a new purpose, and walk with Him through the open doors.

Taprina Milburn's family column, "for Sanity's Sake," is published in *Mature Living* magazine. She is the author of two books, *Scientists Use Rats, I Use My Family* and *We're Not Being Raised Right: And Other Ego-Building Things Kids Say* (to be released December 2011). Her blog is taprinam.wordpress.com.

Ryaja Johnson Rhone

Operation Transforming Freedom

THE RIDE TO the airport was peculiarly quiet. Small talk proved difficult as neither of us knew what to say. Sitting in the terminal, we played a competitive game of UNO to take our minds off the reality of my heading halfway across the world for my first deployment in support of Operation Enduring Freedom.

A voice came over the loud speaker, "We'll now begin boarding." Neither of us moved. We refused to acknowledge we were minutes away from goodbye. Seconds later, or so it seemed, the same voice announced, "This is the final boarding call." We said, "I love you." Then embraced and kissed each other goodbye.

Later, Jamie told me he watched as I handed my plane ticket to the gate agent and disappeared down the jet way. He walked away feeling like his heart was being ripped out of his chest. He did not want to think about his new life as the *spouse left behind*. He tried to keep busy. At the office, he asked his supervisor for additional work. When the work day ended, he doubled his usual time spent in the gym.

Jamie's busy lifestyle and our constant email communication did little to dull his pain of separation. One day he called to say, "Good night." When I answered the phone, he sounded excited just to hear my voice. My work day had barely started and things were already hectic. I did not want to chat just for the sake of chatting. Jamie quickly sensed I was distracted and uninterested. His excitement waned and was replaced with annoyance.

"I'm frustrated right now! I have no idea what I did or said to irritate you," he snapped. "I understand that you work twelve hours a day, six days a week, but that doesn't mean you have the right to lose sight of your accountability to our relationship."

His sudden change in demeanor caught me off guard. I figured I would let him vent so I remained silent.

He continued, "If I call and it's not a good time to chat, let me know! If there's something wrong that we need to talk about, let me know! If you're upset about the weather or anything that lends itself to a crummy conversation, let me know! I'd rather you tell me it isn't a good time to talk."

I was in no mood for confrontation, so I let our conversation conclude with his tirade. I said, "I'll talk to you later, bye," and hung up the phone.

When work slowed, I took inventory of my behavior. I realized it was not the first time I was dismissive. I lost perspective of the importance of family during hectic, high stress times. I knew I could be more attentive, patient, and understanding. Being able to talk to Jamie was a privilege, and I did not want to take it, or him, for granted. Jamie's support, encouragement, and love were getting me through my deployment. That awareness led me to call the next day to apologize.

"Forgive me," I said. "I understand your frustration. I want you to know that I'm not trying to be unemotional or distant. This environment is very stressful. My behavior wasn't aimed at you." I jokingly added, "But, you need to get a hobby. Stop sitting at home crying over me. Join a support group, cry with them." His laughter let me know I was forgiven.

In various forms, tones, and volumes, this scene repeated itself several times. Basic communication, which was easy at home, proved extremely difficult. Interactions, via email and telephone, were marred by misunderstanding, frustration, and impatience. We were constantly reminded of the communication challenges associated with being separated.

Something had to change. We agreed to say a prayer before writing an email or dialing a telephone number. We asked God to bless all our interactions. We learned to ask each other for forgiveness. Humility drew us together in spite of our stubborn pride threatening to push us apart.

In time, we discovered the transforming freedom of our prayers. When God became the focus of our interactions, we were set free from the misunderstanding, frustration, and impatience that plagued us. Our simple act of praying brought us closer and strengthened our marriage in ways I had not expected.

Experience the transforming freedom for yourself—let God be the author, editor, and arbitrator of your speech.

Ryaja Johnson Rhone is a lover of Jesus Christ and author of *Chronicles of an Airman: Discovering Purpose 6,500 Miles from Home* (www.coaabook.com). Ryaja's passion to serve led her from serving her country to serving her community. She now devotes time, talent, and resources to serving those in need.

Joe Márquez-West

Grasping the Awesomeness of God's Plan

HOW FAR ARE we willing to go for God? We've all heard it before, sitting in church or at some Christian revival conference. The high-profile pastor gets up, gets going, and tells us we all need to be transformed, to embrace the Father and the Son and the Holy Ghost and turn our lives around for Jesus. We feel moved in our hearts, raise our hands, and sing with the music. Once the service is over we pray with the nice people with name tags and leave. For a few days, we really try to live godly lives, but soon the matchstick burns out and we are left the same lukewarm Christians doing absolutely nothing of value in this world. Is this transformation?

It's amazing how many Christians go to church every week. Yet, when one looks at the real world, where are all the Christians? Our influence is very hard to see in this dark society. It is clear that something is wrong. If that many people are living transformed lives, why are they making such a small impact on the world? Is it possible that real transformation hasn't taken place?

What is actually the main focus of our lives? Afraid to look like we aren't close with God, we say with our mouths that He is our priority. However, our actions show God isn't first in our lives. Instead of spending our time covering up our apathy, let's ask ourselves what the world would look like if we lived up to Jesus' example? What could we be for God?

Sadly, we don't take the Bible's command to be transformed seriously. Nowadays, a good Christian is somebody who goes to church, consumes Christian media, and stays away from the major sins. Really? That's all it takes? Living for Jesus has turned into not watching R-rated movies, not listening to music with trashy lyrics, and not partying or doing drugs. The differences between Christians and non-Christians pretty much ends there. Some Christians don't even do that much. Yet, somehow, even with the bar set this low, it seems that all we do is whine about how tough it is to be a Christian.

How then can we snap out of this American Christian delusion and live real, transformed lives? Maybe trying an eternal perspective would help. We act as if this life is all there is. However, at this very moment, we are closer to death than ever before. Have you ever sat and thought about this? For all the things you can control in your life, death is not one of them. This is absolutely concrete. One day we will all die.

It's interesting how our conversations center around what we are doing in this life. If we have an eternal perspective, we should be more concerned with life after death. Our future in heaven needs to be real enough to us that it affects our everyday lives. This can be very difficult in a world obsessed with having everything right away. As Christians, we need to understand that we must remove ourselves from this mindset to be truly transformed. Jesus' offer of salvation is not simply a ticket into heaven. Rather, it is a lifetime commitment to active participation in God's transformation of our lives. But instead, we use grace as an excuse to join in with the rest of the world. We forget we are going to have to give an account before a Holy God about our actions on earth. If we realized the brevity of our lives, we'd use our time better, storing up treasures in heaven, and helping others while on earth.

God placed us in the perfect time and place to serve Him best. He gave us every talent we need to fulfill our purpose. God engineered us to help others in a way nobody else can. Let that empower us. God wants us to succeed, so why would we want to do anything other than serve Him? It's what we're created for! If you capture the awesomeness of God's plan, the only thing that makes sense is to give Him your life. Completely rethink your entire worldview. Dismantle your old thoughts and priorities. Destroy what you thought mattered most, and allow God to truly transform your life.

Joe Márquez-West is an exciting guy who loves people. He lives in Aurora, Colorado, with his awesome mom and his fantastic sister. Joe drives a twenty-one year old car, plays guitar, and wishes he could back flip. He is a high school senior graduating with the class of 2012.

Marilyn J. Stewart

You Can't Drink Grapes

MY HUSBAND HAD emergency surgery in the middle of the night, but was doing well now and resting comfortably. I'd gone thirty-nine hours without sleep and was finally headed home.

As I drove the deserted streets of New Orleans, I switched on the wipers to clear the rain from the windshield as the outer bands of tropical storm Lee drifted in. I wasn't worried. I had survived hurricane Katrina and could handle whatever punch Lee had, even if my husband wasn't there to face it with me.

The house was dark as I pulled into the driveway. It was already late and I couldn't wait to go inside, take a hot shower, and slide into my own bed. I pushed the button on the garage door opener, but nothing happened.

The battery must be dead, I thought.

Rain pelted my shoulders and the wind swirled my hair into my face as I opened the car door and dug in the bottom of my purse for my house key. The key slid into the lock, but wouldn't turn. I stared at the key in my hand. Yes, I had the right key. I tried again. On the third try, I lifted the doorknob, but nothing happened. I grabbed the mail from the mailbox and stepped back into the rain, feeling along the fence for the latch to the side gate, and stumbled to the unlocked back door.

Finally inside, I dropped my things on the couch and plopped into the recliner to thumb through the mail. Great. More bills. I sighed. Dollar signs popped in my mind as I mentally did a quick tally of my husband's tab which included an emergency room visit, surgery, and a five-day hospital stay.

I rubbed my neck as I turned on the shower. Stepping in, I yanked my foot back with a yelp. Cold. Even the hot water heater had let me down. *I probably can't get anyone to fix it until*

Monday, I thought with a sigh. I dressed, wrapped myself in a blanket, sat on the couch, and turned on the television to relax.

Then the phone rang.

"Mom?" It was my son calling from graduate school, hundreds of miles away. "There's a mix-up at the registrar's office, and I need my original birth certificate right away." His voice was frantic. The glitch was serious, and his scholarship and a year's worth of work might be at stake.

"Okay. When?"

"Classes start Tuesday," he said. "I need it Monday."

My heart sank. It was Labor Day weekend and mail services, including overnight services, didn't deliver on holidays. My insides were in knots, and all I could do was squeak out a weak prayer.

After we hung up, I paced the living room floor. I'd made it through my husband's health scare. Now, all I had wanted to do was relax. But nothing had gone right from the moment I pulled into the driveway.

My eyes drifted around the living room as I complained out loud to God. The memories of the first time I'd stepped into that room after Hurricane Katrina and saw everything we owned covered in mold came rushing back.

For a year we moved from place to place as our gutted house was rebuilt. Katrina disrupted our world, but the ripple effects eventually touched every aspect of our lives. As I thought about the storm, I remembered what God had done and how he had changed our heartache into joy.

I walked to the bookcase and picked up an old favorite by the great devotional writer Oswald Chambers. The day's reading said: "You cannot drink grapes. Grapes become wine only when they have been squeezed."

It's only when we are broken that we can be of service to others. Sometimes God works through crushing heartache to pull us close to Him. Sometimes He uses the everyday annoyances of life to refine us. I relaxed as I once again made a commitment to let God do it His way as He made me into the person I needed to be. And once again, I felt His sweet comfort.

I am learning that a tested faith transforms, and that God is always at work, always there, and always aware of my need.

Marilyn J. Stewart is a contributing writer to The Times-Picayune of New Orleans and a regional reporter for The Baptist Message, the news journal of Louisiana Baptists. Her articles have appeared in various Baptist publications and in CLASS anthologies.

Lee Warren

Turkeys, Coffee, and the Power of Sacrificial Giving

HEY, I HAVE an idea about Christmas gifts this year," I said. Two of my single guy friends and I talked as we hung out at a coffee shop one cool, fall evening several years ago.

"A couple of days ago, I heard the Open Door Mission is in desperate need of turkeys, coffee, and other food items. What do you guys think about throwing in $20.00 each to buy supplies for the mission instead of exchanging gifts this year?"

One of the guys in our group, John, doesn't like to shop for Christmas presents. He says he doesn't know what to buy and actually experiences stress from the process. I've never understood his dilemma, since we buy each other the same lame gifts every year, but rather than seeing a friend fret, I started thinking we should just forgo the gift exchange. That's when the idea hit me. Rather than buying for each other, we could meet the needs of others.

"I love it," Bob said.

"Let's do it," John said.

We met at a grocery store and piled our cart full of turkeys, coffee, and other items. We spent more than the designated amount, but none of us seemed to care. The idea of giving a gift that would actually help somebody far surpassed the plan to spend only sixty dollars.

After dropping off the food at the mission, we slipped back into the car in silence. I can only describe it as a holy moment—one of those times when you know that the Spirit of God is changing you and changing your perspective. After a couple of minutes, Bob spoke up.

"We should do this every year," he said. "It is so much more fulfilling."

A new tradition was born. We start looking forward to it as early as October. And even though we are just three ordinary single guys with limited resources, we somehow feel different each year after we've experienced the power of giving.

As the years rolled by, we changed things up. Some years the mission needed diapers, other years they needed food. By the way, if you ever want a good belly laugh, watch three single guys walk into a Target and try to figure out the number system on the diaper packaging. Thankfully, a woman saw us struggling to figure it out and came to our rescue.

Two years ago, the mission's website said they had a desperate need for turkeys and everything that goes with them. Bob sent out an email to his co-workers to ask if they wanted to chip in. Then he started calling various supermarkets asking if they'd give us a discount. By the time we headed to the grocery story, we had $225.00 and a 5% discount.

We stacked one shopping cart full of fifteen turkeys and another full of green beans, mashed potato mix, coffee, cranberries, and anything else we thought might go well with a Christmas Day feast.

"I've never seen anybody buy so many turkeys at once," said the clerk who checked us out. We took every turkey the store had in stock and we had just enough money to cover everything. God was at work before we were.

We pulled up to the mission and went inside to see if we could get a cart to take the food in. A man who said he was going through the mission's New Life program brought a cart out for us and we filled it up.

"Come on back in," said the man after we were done. "Meet the chef."

Before we did that, we helped him store the turkeys in the walk-in freezer. We slid the turkeys onto the racks and they looked pretty lonely.

As we chatted with the chef, my thoughts were on the nearly empty freezer. It was hard not to be discouraged, but God seemed to say to me, "Just do your part. I'm in control. If I can feed 5,000 people with two fish and five loaves, then surely I can feed as many people as I want to with fifteen turkeys."

Armed with a new outlook, I couldn't wait to do it all again next year.

Lee Warren is the author of five nonfiction books and has written hundreds of articles for magazines and newspapers. He is also a freelance editor for WinePress Publishing and he owns Christian Manuscript Editing Services (www.christianmanuscriptediting.com) where he offers editing and critique services.

Judy McLaughlin

Abundant Life

I started as a twinkle in my father's eye,
when my mother joined him, so full of life.
A baby born!
She grew, learned to laugh and cry,
her future uncertain, decisions that led to strife.

As a young child, the streets were clear and safe to roam.
At school, was taught and then walked home.
Friends abounded and life was good.
My life was full and I had no care.
I learned to be free, to grow, and share.

A wonderful family, a pampered child.
Oh what more could there be?
My brother, so full of concern,
Introduced me to godly folk.
"What is this?" and then "It is He! It is He!"

A young life changed in the blink of an eye,
I met my Savior, walked in His presence, my head held high.

Transformed

What will be on the road ahead?
What is the journey?
Where will life lead?

God has a plan and has called me by name.
Will I have fortune, will I have fame?

The years go by, youth seems to vanish.
She springs into action.
The call of a young man appears and won the attraction.

Marriage and then a baby; plans for her future.
This family of Dad, Mom, and child have come full circle.
Now it's time to sit still, be open for change,
Hear God's voice, and take a stand.

My life years have come; forget the past.
I continue to prosper.

My Lord blessed me with healing, knowledge, and direction through His whisper.
One who started as a twinkle is now a white-haired, purple-banged saint, and still able to endure.

Transformed from child so full of desires,
I was part of the world and all its sin.
I fell on my knees, when I heard the Lord's voice.
He called me by name and held out His hands.
I reached up, took hold, and rose to follow.
Without doubt, I'm certain I made the right choice.

Judy McLaughlin is a Bible study leader and Certified Personality Trainer. When not volunteering at her church, she can be found working behind the scenes for CLASSEMINARS, Inc. or winning bowling tournaments. She and her husband, Jerry, have been married for fifty-five years and have one daughter, Gayleen. Judy loves to encourage others and help them in their walk with the Lord.

Lisa Ragland

A Life Transformed

I IMMEDIATELY NOTICED her as she walked into the building with her head down, not making eye contact with anybody. She looked angry. I was leading the group she participated in that night. I learned she was there against her will. Her therapist suggested she participate in the Christ-centered recovery program our church offers. The program deals with addictions, hurts, habits, and hang-ups.

Heavily pierced and tattooed, she was definitely different. She obviously did not want to be there, but she vowed to give it a year.

I watched her every Monday night; she was faithful to be there. We did not talk much the first few months. I saw her coming to church on Sunday. She tried not to be noticed, but that was impossible.

About seven months into the program, she asked me to be her accountability partner. God prompted me immediately to say yes. This partnership began the journey for a lifelong friendship.

After our first meeting, I knew I was in over my head. I wondered why God put us together because our paths were so different. I tried not to show my shock as she shared. Her story started at an early age. When most girls are still playing with dolls, she was molested at a church gathering. Her parents did not believe her.

Then at eight, her brother died in a car accident. He was only eighteen. Her dad left. Her mom would not get out of bed. She was on her own. She went to neighbors' houses to get food to eat.

In her teens, she was coerced into a relationship with a guy who led her into a dark, evil lifestyle. She believed God could never love her because of the way she was living and accepted she would go to hell. She even had a demon applied in the form of scarification. There was no going back on the process.

After years of making wrong choices and many suicidal thoughts, she sought counseling.

She faced lots of heartache during the process of letting go of the past and learning that the past did not define who she was. She cried a lot of healing tears.

Several months into the program, she gave her life to Christ and the real transformation took place. She faced issues head on instead of running from them, as she used to do. She started a daily relationship with God.

While she managed being bipolar, depression and thoughts of suicide were becoming part of her past as she lived her life in Christ. The closer she got to Christ the more she radiated the love of the Lord. She started giving back. She plugged in to church and started serving. I remember when I encouraged her to serve. She picked the greeting ministry, hoping to avoid serving because of the piercing in her nose. When selected, she started greeting. Some people came to church because of her. She gradually removed her piercings as she became more God-centered and less self-centered. The piercings no longer defined her.

She then started studying God's Word and prayed for His guidance every day. I soon noticed if she had a down day, it only lasted for a day. In the past, she would have been depressed for a week or a month.

God has transformed her into one of the strongest women I know because she let Him. He called her into ministry. She is in seminary and wants to work with women. I know her future is bright because I know God is guiding her. "Do not conform any longer to the pattern of this world, but be transformed by the renewing of your mind. Then you will be able to test and approve what God's will is—His good, pleasing and perfect will" (Romans 12:2 NIV).

When she allowed God to change her heart, she became a life transformed.

Lisa Ragland and her husband, Mike, live in Dickinson, Texas. She has a passion for her family. Lisa has three grown children and four grandchildren. She loves writing, speaking, and encouraging others. She has a published article in *Out of The Overflow*. You can follow her blog at www.lisaragland.blogspot.com.

Gary Chevalier

Galvanized

HURRICANE ALICIA ROARED through southeast Texas in the late summer of 1983, leaving massive destruction in her wake. Hundreds of people lost their lives. Countless homes and businesses were destroyed. The hurricane crippled roads, power lines, and other infrastructure, disrupting life for years to come. Though God spared our house from storm damage, the rest of our property didn't fare as well. About thirty trees blew over on our little acre and a half in the shadow of Houston, Texas, and anything on which they fell was likewise destroyed.

Of all the things we lost which were important to me, by far my greatest lament was over the tree that held our basketball goal. It was a proud oak tree at the rear of the property, so thick that when my brother and I bear-hugged it at the same time, we couldn't wrap our arms far enough around to touch each other's fingers. As a young teenage boy, my world revolved around playing basketball in the back yard, and I was distraught over the loss. Something else that perished in the hurricane was our swing set. It was one of those old-school, "built-to-last," A-frame structures made out of galvanized steel. Nevertheless, the massive oak tree crashed down and buckled the swing set like pipe cleaners at a craft fair. Everything in our back yard had been rendered completely worthless or so I thought. My dad, you see, is absolutely masterful at "repurposing" items. To this day I still marvel at how he took the twisted wreckage of that swing set and crafted it into the coolest free-standing basketball goal in the neighborhood. He placed it in a shaded, flat spot with little grass and the new goal created hours upon hours of fun for my friends and me in the years to come. Every time I go to my parent's house, the galvanized steel structure still proudly reigns over its corner in the back yard. I never saw the potential of that mangled steel to be anything other than the swing set it had been, but my father did.

I have recently experienced my own repurposing by my heavenly Father. The first seventeen years of my post-college career were spent as a worship pastor. Through God's favor and a lot

47

of work, I learned a lot; God used me to transform our worship services and help grow our church exponentially. I never saw myself as anything but a worship pastor. I loved what I was doing, loved doing it with God's people, and planned to make no changes until I retired. God's new direction for me, however, slowly began to creep into my periphery and over a matter of months, He made it clear to me that my time in worship ministry was nearing an end. He began to open doors for me in the marriage and family realm. Though I knew it was the direction He was leading me, I was living in a "Moses moment," paralyzed by fear and an inability to see down the path to which He was calling me. Then, God dropped an oak of change onto my plans and like the swing set, I crumpled.

God, however, is the master at re-purposing. He knew what I had been, but He also saw what I could be and awoke in me a passion and a desire to grow families. He had already given me the gifts to do it, but I rarely had the opportunity to exercise them because of my role as a worship pastor. In my new reality, though, those hindrances are gone and I am poised to stand tall and make an impact! Praise God He saw through the wreckage of my plans and He didn't ship me off to the scrap heap. Rather, He molded me into something new that would serve His purposes.

In Jeremiah 18:3-4, God speaks about the potter and the clay. He reminds us that like the potter, He can and will remold us into something useful for His purposes. This process is often painful, but it's an exercise in trust, in obedience, in faith; but more than these, it's an exercise in hope. Hope no matter how tangled, bent, broken, and worthless our lives or our plans, God sees only the beauty of a shiny, new basketball goal.

Gary Chevalier is a husband, father, and a family relationship specialist. His role as a K-12 school principal empowers him to work with a large number of students and families, and he and his wife routinely speak at church events, marriage retreats, and more. www.garychevalier.com

Amy Wyatt

The Light in His Eyes

IT'S HOT, HOT!" my daddy rasped. Doctors had just removed the ventilator that sustained his breathing for the past 48 hours. After being told not to expect him to breathe on his own, we were shocked he was talking.

My husband and I shared a glance over the words my father spoke. My mother was convinced he said "right" as in "it's all right," but we both feared something in the spiritual realm was happening. I thought my daddy was going to hell.

My mom married my stepdad when I was in the second grade. He was in the Navy and gave new meaning to the phrase "cuss like a sailor." He was a good man, but he never went to church, not even on Christmas or Easter. His weekends were spent drinking beer and watching NASCAR. He didn't even pray over meals.

I knew my father didn't know Christ. When he was sedated and vented I wondered if I had lost my chance to tell him, once again, that God loved him. I stood over his bed reading scripture. I fervently prayed for his soul and his life. I was terrified my prayers had gone unanswered.

Over the next 24 hours, we watched and waited. The doctors told us not to expect much. When you're diagnosed with stage 3 lung cancer, there isn't much hope. The projected life expectancy is six to eighteen months, even with treatment. When he developed pneumonia and landed in the hospital, the doctor said he wasn't strong enough to start chemotherapy.

We called family and friends. Mark, one of my dad's closest childhood friends, came to visit. I sat Daddy up so he could talk. "Mark," he whispered, "I've known you my whole life. I'm not going to shove this down your throat, but I have to tell you something. God loves you. He has a plan for your life. He knew all of your days before they came to be."

I couldn't believe his words. Scripture. The very scripture I had read aloud just days before as he lay sedated. It was no coincidence. He heard me, proof God's Word does not return void.

Daddy continued, "Mark, I was dying and I was going to hell. But God not only spared my life, he saved my soul. And he loves you too." Mark sat there speechless, but I knew my dad made an impact.

Mark's wife called my mom the next Sunday afternoon. Mark had gone to church with her that morning for the first time in a long time.

I watched, amazed, as my daddy, the man I feared was going to hell, began to tell all who visited him about the love of God. He was a changed man.

After two weeks in hospice, my father went home. "Hospice isn't a place for the living," a nurse told us as he was released. When he recovered from the pneumonia, he was strong enough to begin treatments, chemotherapy, and then radiation.

Over the next several months, his body deteriorated. He lost all his hair and almost 100 pounds. You could see the bones beneath his skin. Some days, he could barely walk, or sit up, but insisted on attending church on Sunday, a practice never important to him before. Every time I visited, his Bible was open on the kitchen table, where he studied Scripture. Though his cheeks were sunken and all of his facial hair gone, the Light in his eyes couldn't be extinguished.

I watched a burly, bearded, broad-shouldered man dwindle to a weakling, but at the same time saw the formation of a spiritual giant; a man physically withering, but spiritually thriving.

But isn't that the way God works? At our weakest, He shows Himself strong, if we will only allow Him to step in and transform us.

Amy Wyatt is a speaker, Bible study teacher, freelance writer, and daddy's girl. She travels the country as an epilepsy advocate educating those whose lives have been touched by epilepsy. She is a regular devotional contributor to Five Minutes for Faith and the Presidential Prayer Team. Find her at www.signsmiraclesandwonders.blogspot.com.

Sandra Herron

A Pocket Parable: An Eraser and Thirty-seven Cents

WHAT DID YOU hide in your pocket when you were a kid? What do you keep in your pockets today? Perhaps there is a treasure stuffed into your pocket right now!

There was never a little boy more anxious to please his grandfather than Lance. The family birthday party with cake and gifts was not enough for Lance. He was a big boy now. He was three years old and he wanted to give his own present.

As little boys will do, Lance always had pockets full of junk, including erasers. For some reason, he dearly loved erasers. He thought it was magical the way an eraser could make pencil marks and even finger prints on the walls disappear.

Poppa was engrossed in the newspaper. "Poppa, look. Happy birthday, Poppa. I have my own present for you." Poppa lowered the paper and looked over the top of his glasses. Lance reached down deep into the pocket of his patched Levis© and struggled to pull out a tiny gift wrapped in Kleenex® and a rubber band twisted into a bow. "It's for you Poppa. It's my best eraser. 'Cause, Poppa, I really love you."

Then Lance's little freckled face broke into a huge grin. "I have something else for you Poppa, 'cause I love you." He struggled again to reach down to the bottom of his Levis© pocket. He pulled his chubby dimpled hand out and revealed some coins. "Here Poppa, you can have all my money. This is all the money I've got and it's for you Poppa. Happy birthday."

Now tears are sneaking their way down Poppa's cheek. "Oh, Lance, I can't take all your money."

"Yeah, Poppa, it's for you 'cause you are my Poppa and I love you. Is it lots of money, Poppa? How much is it?"

"Oh yes, it's lots of money Lance. It's thirty-seven cents. Thank you very, very much." Lance jumped up and down in place three times grinning from ear to ear.

Transformed

An eraser and thirty-seven cents seems like a small gift, but it was everything to Lance. It was everything to Poppa. The simple act of unreserved giving brought heaven to earth in one stunning moment. A sweaty dimpled little hand revealed a glimpse of God.

Who do you love enough to give everything to? Everything you have in the pockets of your life? Has anyone ever given everything they had for you?

Missionary Jim Elliott said: "He is no fool who gives what he cannot keep to gain what he cannot lose." Well, Jesus gave His all when He gave His life for you. As He surrendered His life, He erased all your mistakes and misdeeds simply because He loves you.

Dr. Sandra Herron considers herself a personal alchemist, not working with metals, but with people. She renders out the negative preconceived beliefs and worldly labels and brings forth the gold that is within. There is always gold within. We are creations of God, created in His image which is gold of the best kind.

Candy Arrington

Mind and Body Transformation

SEVERAL MONTHS AGO, I embarked on a personal weight loss campaign. This wasn't my first endeavor, but I hope it will be my last. Over the years, I've tried many methods of losing weight and keeping it off, but this time, I realized I was going to have to change my mind along with my body.

In the past, my attitude has always centered on doing as little as possible to get the desired results, feeling that once I reached my weight loss goal, I could eat as I pleased. Not surprisingly, the numbers on the scale always crept up again.

This time, I've taken a different approach. I asked God to help me examine the way I think about food and discovered several things: I equate food with comfort; I view food as reward; I usually eat "bad" foods when I am by myself, therefore, preserving the illusion that I am careful about what I eat; and I eat certain foods when I don't really want them so I can get them before someone else does. The last revelation was the hardest to face because it forced me to admit I am selfish.

It was somewhat of a comfort to realize I am not the only one to struggle with the "me" problem. Peter thought himself capable of enduring all Jesus faced, but when it came down to self-preservation, he denied association with his Lord. James and John, the "sons of thunder," wanted places of prominence in heaven on either side of Christ. The rich young ruler sought eternal life, but didn't want to change his social status or give up his wealth to attain it. With these in mind, and others, I took a look at what I needed to do to shift my me-focus and change the way I thought about food.

First, I gave up the excuse that I didn't have time to exercise more than the cursory amount of time I'd always allotted for that activity—forty-five minutes, three times a week. When I examined the number of hours I wasted in a week on other things—watching television, talking on the phone, time online—I realized more time was available for exercise, but I squandered it on meaningless activities. I increased the number of days I exercise to five, then to seven, and made it my goal to walk 10,000 steps a day, the equivalent of about five miles. Some of this I accomplished in the gym, the rest pounding the pavement.

Second, I worked on changing the way I view food. I began to think of it as fuel for my body rather than comfort, reward, or acquisition. Formerly, when on a diet, certain foods were off limits. This time, I allowed any food as long as it fit in my prescribed calorie allotment for the day. I soon discovered it wasn't worth it to eat a high calorie pastry if it meant I had no calories left by suppertime or I had to walk another two miles to compensate. And I faced the undeniable fact that when I cheat, and eat more than my body needs for fuel, I can't hide the effect on my body. I wear that sneaked cookie or extra serving for all to see.

Third, with God's prompting, I examined myself through a spiritual microscope, which was incredibly hard to do. I began to notice other ways I am selfish and made adjustments to shift my focus outward rather than inward. I incorporated more spiritual training into my life the same way I employed physical and mental discipline. Amazingly, the combination of spirit, mind, and body transformed my attitude about not only me, but many other things as well. I'm not sure why I was surprised. Scripture clearly tells us all three are involved—mind, soul, and strength (Mark 12:30). In some ways, my initial goal, weight loss, became only a minor part of change. My overall perspective on food, exercise, selfishness, and discipline shifted and I pray the changes will last longer than a season. I believe it is a life change, a life transformation.

When we accept Jesus as Savior, we become new creations in Him. In the same way, when we examine things in our lives that replace Him as Lord, and adjust those things, we move closer to becoming more like Him.

Candy Arrington's publishing credits include *Writer's Digest, The Writer, Thriving Family, The Lookout, Encounter,* and *Chicken Soup.* She is coauthor of *When Your Aging Parent Needs Care: Practical Help for this Season of Life* (Harvest House) and *AFTERSHOCK: Help, Hope, and Healing in the Wake of Suicide* (B&H Publishing Group).

Linda Gilden

I Am Really, Really Old

FOUR-YEAR-OLD TREY TOOK my face in his hands and squeezed as he pulled me close to him. "Rose, you are *really, really* old!"

Caught a little off guard, I just smiled at him. He wouldn't really want to know what I thought about that remark!

Getting even closer, so our noses almost touched, he smiled, and with a twinkle in his eye, said, "But we won't tell anybody."

Never one to dwell on age, it didn't matter to me who knew how "really, really old" I was. But to a lot of people, it is important to keep track as the years pass.

Many friends marked milestone birthdays with elegant parties, skydiving experiences, and trips around the world. Not a party person or particularly adventurous, what does getting older look like to me?

Age is not chronological. Despite the increasing number of candles on my birthday cake, I choose to enjoy each year as it comes and count it as a blessing, not something to dread.

One of the things that comes with getting older is an increased comfort level with myself. At some point, I realized God created me to fill a special spot in His plan, one no one else could fill. Thus, the competition in life diminished and I was free to enjoy my friends and family without concern about what I did. My spot was already there and those around me couldn't take it away. How comforting.

This realization translated into everything I did. When I write a book, I don't have to worry that someone else may write that book or whether an acquisitions editor will get that book from someone else. Mine is unique. And as I search for the right place for it, I meet many wonderful people along the way, people who will allow me to be me!

Along with my growing self-assurance came fewer thoughts about what others think. Oh, I still want to make a good impression because in everything I do I am an ambassador of the King. But as long as He is okay with what I do, that is all that matters.

Probably the biggest benefit to getting "really, really old" is the spiritual growth I have experienced. My expectation about what is to come is different. I read my Bible and take the messages to heart with a new anticipation. When I worship, the connection seems stronger, the line more direct. Fellowship with those who have the same perspective encourages and uplifts me.

Lest you think that one day I just woke up and bounced out of bed with this perspective, I did not. God has been teaching me for over half a century. For some things, I caught on pretty quickly, but in other ways I have been a slow learner. He has sent difficult lessons where there was no option but to sit in His lap and let Him teach me. In all ways, He has been changing and growing me into the person He wants me to be.

Am I sitting around with my bags packed, waiting for the heavenly bus to get to my stop? Absolutely not! My life is full and every day brings sweet surprises.

Does it really matter to me if Trey tells everybody how old I am? Not a bit. While my younger years were fun and full, I am finding times are even better when you are "really, really old!"

Linda Gilden is an author, speaker, editor, and writing coach. She is the Director of the CLASS Christian Writers Conference and loves to inspire you to encourage those you love. She is the author of the popular *Love Notes* series and *Mommy Pick-Me-Ups*. Linda lives in South Carolina with her husband, three adult children and their families, which include the four cutest grandchildren in the world.

Esi Mathis

Just One Question

AS I STEPPED from the shower, a sudden pain pierced my right jaw. I felt like something had slammed into my head. I froze, holding my face, unsure of what was coming next.

On November 9, 2009, the day after returning from a rich, wonderful experience at the CLASS Christian Writers Conference in Abiquiu, New Mexico, I came face-to-face with the prospect of my own death. Sensing something was terribly wrong, I called three people: my landlord, Patti; a local friend, Wendy; and a South Carolina friend, Bernestine. Although I knew the pain in my head was not the familiar migraine, I didn't recognize it as a 9-1-1 situation.

After hours of painful uncertainty, I heard the quiet, distinctive voice of God instructing me to take a simple life-saving action. Three hours after the onset of what I later learned was a brain aneurysm, I was still alive even after falling asleep for two hours. This alone has been a death sentence for countless victims.

If I could just go to bed, I thought, I will feel better in the morning. Just as I pulled the white cotton blanket away from my pillow, the Lord whispered, "Call the hospital."

The hospital? Looking around the room, I searched for the scrap of paper where I had written the phone number for Methodist Hospital. "How can I help you?" the woman at Methodist Hospital asked. After I listed my symptoms and the timeline, she asked, "How old are you?"

When she learned I was 55, she said, "You need to get here right away." I called the number she gave me for a local taxi. I managed to dress and slowly make my way to the waiting taxi.

After four days in Methodist Hospital, I was transferred to Huntington Hospital in Pasadena for brain surgery. Later I learned family and friends had bombarded heaven with many questions, some asked in anger. Yet, I had just one question for God.

Standing in the doorway of my bathroom where the dreaded incident occurred, I said, "Lord, many people who love me are very upset with you right now. They don't understand

57

why this happened to me, and they are asking why You allowed it. My question to You is not why, but what? What do You want to do with this experience for Your glory?"

It is the nature of us, as humans, to question God in moments of uncertainty and despair, asking Him, "Why?" Much has been offered to explain why bad things happen to us, especially when we generally consider ourselves to be "good people." But God uses difficult circumstances to draw us closer to Him.

Esi Mathis, a Florida native, is a Christian Life Coach, freelance writer, and Certified Personality Trainer who lives in southern California. She loves helping people improve their relationships and achieve their goals. Esi can be contacted at esimathis@gmail.com.

Linda Jewell

Supplications on Steroids: Praying for Those You Love

IN 1999, MY soldier-son Ty, served in a hot spot in the Balkans between warring ethnic groups. During a rare overseas phone call, he casually told me about when he and other American soldiers had escorted a relocating group of angry Albanians through a countryside filled with enraged Serbs.

My heart pounding, I thought of what could have happened if Ty had been caught in crossfire of bricks or bullets. My regular prayers seemed puny compared to my new anxieties for my son's safety.

I needed reassurance. In fact, I needed supplications on steroids. I pleaded with God to give me Scripture to pray for my son. I figured His words would be better than anything I could come up with alone.

Serendipitously, within a few days as I read the Bible, God pointed me to Psalm 91. I'd read it many times before, but given Ty's circumstances it held new meaning for me, especially verse five: "You will not fear the terror of the night, nor the arrow that flies by day."

"Thank You, God," I said, "This is exactly what I need to pray for Ty."

Each morning I used Psalm 91 as a prayer. Whenever my anxiety level rose after watching grim news reports or when I hadn't heard from my son for a while, I grabbed my Bible and flipped it open to Psalm 91, and prayed for Ty.

However, in the middle of dark nights when I startled awake, I'd do the time-zone math. Wondering what he was doing at that moment, I'd become fearful again for my son's safety. I needed instant recall of the Scripture. I didn't want to wake my sleeping husband by getting out of bed or turning on the light to read my Bible.

I needed to memorize Psalm 91.

First, I looked at different translations. The Revised Standard Version of the Bible uses the wording "…no scourge come near your tent." These words resonated with me. My son, among the first American soldiers into Kosovo, lived in a tent.

Although memorizing does not come easily, I was a highly motivated mom. I wrote the Psalm longhand many times. Sixteen verses. Two-hundred sixty-six words. Priceless.

I walked around my neighborhood park every morning holding a hand-written copy. I repeated the Scripture line by line, gradually being able to recall more words. I also visualized Psalm 91 as a movie clip with my son finding refuge under God's wings.

It took me three years to memorize Psalm 91. By that time, Ty was serving in yet another part of the world.

I later read that Psalm 91 is known as the Soldier's Prayer. It's an appropriate appeal for our men and women in the military. This Scripture also has served me—a soldier's mom—well as Ty served three years in Europe, one year in Southeast Asia, and three tours in the Middle East.

As a home-front mom, I'll always feel as though I'm holding my emotional breath for the length of my son's deployments. But now I know what to do when I awaken anxiously in the middle of dark nights.

I feel God's power in this prayer. I don't know how Psalm 91 helps my son, but I trust it does. I do know it helps me because it chases my worries away again and again. I give Jesus my anxiety, and He gives me His peace. Sensing God's presence I unclench my jaws and drift back to sleep, assured my son is in God's hands. I trust God gave me the words He wants me to pray for my son. As the Lord of Hosts He is the Commander of His heavenly army. I rest secure because Jesus knows better than I do my son's need for courage and protection while doing his duty. As an added benefit, God gives me His peace, a renewed mind and a transformed life through the power of prayer—supplications on steroids.

Linda Jewell, from Sedona, Arizona, writes and speaks about family matters, patriotism, parenting, and prayer and is published in numerous magazines and compilation books. She serves on The CLASSeminar faculty. Visit www.LindaJewell.com for more information.

Kristen Clark

The Gratitude List

"**P**ERSONALLY," SHE WHISPERED, "I think the reason you have such a miserable life is because you have a bad attitude."

I could always count on Jennifer to tell me what I needed to hear whether I wanted to hear it or not. I had been complaining about my growing mound of bills while failing to celebrate a bonus I had received at work. She quickly realized my problem.

"What you need is an attitude adjustment. You need to develop an attitude of gratitude," she continued.

She was right. I was the Queen of Entitlement and Expectation and had mastered the art of judgment and criticism. I called bank tellers idiots when they asked for my account number the second time. I berated customer service representatives for putting me on hold longer than five minutes. I accused the dry cleaning clerks of sheer stupidity when the spaghetti stain remained evident on my pale pink blouse. I dismissed good friends for not dropping everything to accommodate my needs, and then I complained about them to anyone who would listen. On many days I was outright mean.

As a new Christian, I understood how developing thankfulness was God's will for me. I was undergoing a transformation, one that included developing the same mindset and attitudes as Christ, which meant being prayerful, joyful, and grateful in all circumstances. Unfortunately, I struggled with the part about being grateful.

Thankfully, I have always been motivated by pain and tend to become willing to do something different when I am uncomfortable in a given situation. By this time, I was miserable. I had reached my all-time low—emotionally, physically, mentally, financially, and spiritually.

"Why don't you try keeping a gratitude list," my friend offered. "Write down three things each day that you are grateful for."

61

Transformed

I took her suggestion to heart and began the adventure of writing a daily gratitude list, only I wasn't very good at it. My initial lists were overly simplistic and uncreative or uninspiring:

The roof over my head.

Food in the pantry.

A steady paycheck.

These everyday items were the extent of my gratitude until Jennifer suggested I write down three things I am grateful for each day without listing the same thing twice—*ever!*

Ooh, that was tough! But the added caveat forced me to look more closely at the details of my life, including those things I had taken for granted over the years. The Bible tells us those who seek good will find good, and it didn't take long before I started to understand just how blessed my life really was.

A few months later, I read Proverbs 15:15, which states, "For the poor, every day brings trouble; for the happy heart, life is a continual feast." That single verse resonated deeply in my spirit, and I quickly grabbed my Bible to see what else was written about gratitude and attitude. I was thrilled with what I found.

I read about how attitudes can shape personality and, while we cannot always choose our circumstances, we can choose our attitudes about them and focus on things that are true, pure, and lovely.

Today I am grateful for Jennifer's honesty and willingness to suggest my attitude needed a transformation. With her help, and through daily prayer, I began a journey through which I now see God's numerous blessings in my life. Today, my gratitude list celebrates those blessings:

The teller who asked for my account number the second time as a security measure.

The representative's effort to solve my problem, no matter how long I waited on hold.

The clerk's success in removing most of the evidence of my clumsiness with food.

The grace my friends have shown me over the years and how valuable their friendship is. Ah, life is good!

Kristen Clark continues to maintain her gratitude list and speaks frequently on the topic. Her articles on marriage and relationships have appeared in numerous journals and magazines, and her inspirational stories have appeared in *Chicken Soup for the Soul*. She and her husband Lawrence manage and write for Hiswitness.org and NewBeginningsMarriage.org.

Terry Burns

Parting Thoughts

Brilliant colors on the mesa, morning sun lights it up,
as I sit in the quiet to take it in with my morning coffee cup.
Animals stir all around, as they have throughout the night
but as people arise the animals fade, back away from sight.

A gentle breeze stirs the leaves with a sound like falling rain,
and the leaves on the ground answer back with an echoing refrain.
The Ghost Ranch calls us back, fore we've even had time to go,
or bids us stay as we pack our bags still warming in the glow…

Of a time with friends both old and new, sharing words and sharing souls;
refreshing spirits and strengthening hearts where the world has taken toll.
It's been a trip to an earlier time, a slower pace for sure,
the time to reflect and to learn new things, write words we hope will endure.

It's been a time of quiet reflection, a time to take it in…
The stark beauty God crafted here, a time to newly begin
to set our feet on a brand new path or redirect our minds,
in a manner we came and hoped to do, though of many different kinds…

Of people, ways, and dreams to fill and now with different goals;
formed and nourished through this time in just as many souls.
The conference sends us forth with hope, while it also calls us back…
to finish things we now start and give us what we lack.

Terry Burns writes inspirational fiction, a little poetry, and is an agent with Hartline Literary Agency. He has over forty books in print, including eleven novels, has published several hundred articles and short stories, and been included in over a dozen collections such as this one. A popular speaker at conferences and workshops across the country his available works and his blog can be found at his website www.terryburns.net or the agency site at www.hartlineliterary.com.

Anne Arvizu

A Pivotal Moment

THE FIRST THING I recall was the blood dripping down the right side of my face. It felt warm and I heard the drops thump against the roof of the wreck. I hung upside down, suspended like a bat in the passenger's seatbelt of my best friend's car. The vehicle had spun out of control when Beth had a petit-mal seizure at the wheel. We were propelled headlong into oncoming traffic just before our car hydroplaned and rolled down and over into the embankment. When the little gold car made impact in the ditch, it folded in half like an accordion, and so did I. It took a team of emergency technicians and medics quite a while to pry me out and put me on a stretcher.

The last words out of my mouth as the car spun out of control were not "Oh, My!" They were "Oh," and a word I didn't really want to enter eternity with. I remember praying a nanosecond prayer right before the crash, "Lord, give me a second chance and I'll clean up my mouth." He did.

In one slow motion moment, life as I knew it changed forever.

The combination of the cold rainy night and an unresolved medical condition was not the right mixer that November evening. Throw in the alcohol we had been drinking and it was an accident waiting to happen for my epileptic friend. For many years, I blamed myself. She had just been released to drive after having epilepsy most of her life. It was the first time I had ridden in the car with her. How could I be so stupid? I figured it was my punishment for being disobedient to underage drinking laws, our families, and her doctor.

Careening in and out of consciousness, I remember vivid scenes. First, my mom arrived. Next, I felt the searing pain of being moved from the car and strapped to a board. Then, in the ambulance lying flat and wrapped in white sheets, I could hear some of the not-so-good reports. I passed out to escape the throbbing, which seemed to now envelope my body. Finally, the stark bright lights of the emergency room woke me up just in time to hear the doctor's instructions to the nurse. She prepped me on a cold metal table to shave parts of my head so he could clean the wounds and sew the stitches. For a college sorority girl trying to fit in socially, I remember audibly protesting, "Not the hair," in a weak mumble right before hearing the shaver's buzz. As long blond locks fell to the floor, I blacked out again—a better option to an emotionally painful reality.

Now after two decades, two spinal surgeries, and lots of ongoing doctors appointments, my prayer is, "Lord, let the last words in my heart and from my lips be praise to You." The Bible tells us we will be judged for every idle word we speak. Why even waste breath with filler words like 'um' when God has taught us over and over in Scripture of the life and death power our tongues carry? When we are around others who curse or speak negatively, Paul tells us via the Corinthians what will happen. "Do not be deceived," the Scriptures say, "bad company will corrupt good habits."

I thank God for so many things: I can walk. My heart and my words have lined up with His purpose. And, I am an unashamed worshipper of Jesus, whom I know heard my prayer that dark night.

I can't do what others with healthy spines even twice my age can do. I hear of eighty-year olds running marathons, and as a forty-something, I can't compete. But that crushing circumstance perhaps was no accident at all. God used it to change my spirit and my mouth forever.

Remember Isaiah? When God showed up to him, his first response was, "Woe is me! I am undone, for I am a man of unclean lips." An angel pressed a burning coal to Isaiah's lips so he could be used to speak for the Lord. Today I am more humbled than ever that He would use my mouth as his mouthpiece and my fingers on a keyboard as the pen of His ready writer.

"The tongue of the wise dispenses knowledge, but the mouth of fools pour out folly."
—Proverbs 15:2 NRSV

Founder of Christian Coaching International, (www.GodCoach.com), leadership coach, speaker, and author, Dr. Anne Arvizu empowers leaders to achieve the GodDream™ within. She challenges believers to "walk in a manner worthy of their calling" and to see tripping stones as foundations, mountains as a means to arise, and oceans as an opportunity for water walking.

Gloria Penwell

Silk Purses

"I beseech you therefore brethren, by the mercies of God, that you present your bodies a living sacrifice, holy and acceptable unto God, which is your reasonable service. And be not conformed to this world; but be transformed by the renewing of your mind, that you may prove what is that good and acceptable and perfect will of God."

—Romans 12:1, 2

SANDY AND I scour the flea markets, thrift shops, and garage sales hunting for men's ties. Many women we speak to say their husbands no longer wear ties. Good news for us. They're a marvelous source of inexpensive fabric.

What we do with the ties reminds me of the Romans 12 passage. We take a discarded item, no longer useful or wanted, and transform it into something unique and different.

First, we choose a tie for its color or design. We de-construct it, rip apart the seams and discard the lining. Afterward, it looks like junk, but through the eyes of the seamstress, it's a beautiful thing.

It's very much like we are when we present ourselves to God to be re-made by Him. He may find it necessary to de-construct and rip us apart. It is a painful process in preparation for the beauty He is about to create.

Next, the tie, looking even more like trash, is cut into pieces. The bottom V is retained in its original shape for a flap, but the rest is divided into seven-inch sections. Then something almost magical happens. The sections are sewn together, forming two larger pieces of material. Still rough and unformed, it's beginning to show possibilities.

Many times our lives seem patched and ugly. We've presented ourselves to God to be remade, but we feel as though we're worse off than we were before we made the commitment. We see ourselves as rough and unformed much like the tie fabric at this stage of the process.

In the step that follows we can begin to see a glimpse of the beauty that this "thing" will become. A pattern is laid on the fabric that has been created, and it is cut out.

God uses the Word, preaching, teaching, life experiences, and prayers to form the pattern by which we will be cut.

The sewing together of the patterned pieces begins to show the transformation being done to the tie. All of a sudden, what once was a man's necktie starts to look like a purse.

Once God has our full attention, and He's able to form us into what He wants us to be, He can begin to put the refinements on what we will be for Him. II Corinthians 5:17 says, "Therefore, if anyone is in Christ, he is a new creation. The old is passed away; behold the new has come."

What remains to be done to the purse is to put on the finishing touches. Embellishments, handles, and closures are sewn onto it. Pretty buttons, beads, and crystals are added to the bag, making each one winsome, attractive, and useful.

The finishing touches of our Christian lives are a lifetime of experiences and time spent with the Lord. Amazing things can happen to us when we present ourselves to the God who is our spiritual tailor. He can make something old, unused, and ugly into something beautiful and useful. We just have to ask, and then be ready for the changes He will create in us.

Gloria Penwell has traveled to many Christian writers conferences with her late husband, Dan Penwell. Currently she represents AMG Publishers. She has a love for writers and endeavors to encourage them. She shares a small business, The Ladies from Down Under, making totes and silk purses from discarded ties.

Evelyn Gutierrez

Reaping in the Harvest

"So neither the one who plants nor the one who waters is anything, but only God who makes things grow. The one who plants and the one who waters have one purpose and they will be rewarded according to their own labors."

—Galatians 6:7 MSG

MY FATHER, TOMAS Baca, died fourteen years ago, yet he helped introduce Melissa Hosey to Jesus Christ in September, 2011. No, he didn't return from the grave. He had a passionate heart for helping others, which is something I inherited. I enjoy feeding, praying for, and loving all those in need, especially those seeking God. These longings were also my father's heart's desires.

Melissa was driving aimlessly around the streets of Albuquerque when she saw the Jesus First church sign. It drew her like a magnet. She entered a church for the first time. That day I first met Melissa. Everyone at the church embraced, hugged, and accepted her. After five minutes, she left. She later confided to me that she felt out of place and very uncomfortable in this unfamiliar territory.

The next weekend, Melissa found herself in the same area and was drawn to our Jesus First sign—again. She entered the church and received the same treatment. This time, Melissa stayed a little longer. She was troubled and seeking but didn't know what she was seeking. During the altar call, Melissa responded hoping to find something or someone to fill the void in her life.

Jesus Christ satisfied Melissa. Her love for Him grew more and more daily. She had to tell someone about Jesus and her love for Him. She did! Melissa began telling everybody she came into contact with about Jesus Christ. What my dad Tomas Baca had passed along to me, I had passed to Melissa. Now she was passing along her love for Jesus to others. Melissa wrote the poem below to describe the change in her life.

Transformation
by
Melissa Hosey

Go ahead and try to test
What God's will is for your best
He knows which way you step
Either with your right or your left.

Romans 12:2 says, "Do not conform
But be transformed
By renewing your mind
Even if we have to be kind

It's a thing that day by day
What more does the Bible say?

Go ahead and try to test
What God's will is for your best
He knows which way you step
Either with your right or with your left.

We come from all walks of life
And even different kinds of strife.

But the Word of God brought us here
Without a sigh or a tear
To change every heart from finish to start
Please listen to me
So you can see
How you can be transformed
By everything God can do.

Reaping in the Harvest

Tomas Baca didn't personally know Melissa Hosey or plant the seed but is reaping in the harvest.

Evelyn Gutierrez has served as a book table volunteer for the CLASS Christian Writers Conference for four years. She has managed the Tomas Baca Food Pantry for the last sixteen years. When not volunteering, she provides daycare for her six grandchildren. Evelyn and her husband, Gilbert, have two daughters.

The Day I Lost It

George Porter

IN SEPTEMBER 1972, I began my first year of teaching junior high students in a small northeast Texas town. Excited about the start of school, I wasn't worried about taking on my first year. Maybe that should have been the first clue trouble was headed in my direction.

I realized my biggest problem might be in the area of student discipline. One student, whom I'll call Bobby, made life miserable. Bobby had his own agenda for behavior and many of the class members followed his lead. He had some natural leadership qualities, just headed in the wrong way. I felt totally prepared to handle the science curriculum, but Bobby's behavior, not so much. No matter what I asked the class to do, Bobby found some sneaky way to disrupt the entire class.

Even before the end of the first semester, I realized I wouldn't survive if some drastic measures were not taken to eliminate the misbehavior of little Bobby. That day came much sooner rather than later. As Bobby sat in mid-morning science class, defying anything I asked of him, I decided I had reached my limit. My colleague next door happened to be available, so I asked if he would sit with my class while I addressed "my problem."

Looking across the room and locking eyes with Bobby, I motioned for him to follow me. We made our way down the hall, outside, and out behind the gym. I took off my coat, laid it on the ground, and loosened my tie. Bobby became a little more wide-eyed as he shifted his weight from one foot to the other.

"Bobby, you have done nothing but give me a hard time since this school year began. I have had enough and now it's time for this to end." I leaned forward and extended my jaw slightly. "I'll let you take the first blow, but you better make sure it's your best. Then, it will be my turn and I will lay you out flat."

By this time he was ghostly white and his eyes as big as dinner plates. He took a couple of steps backward and replied, "Mr. Porter, I really don't want to do this." His voice cracked and squeaked as if he wasn't sure what would be an acceptable tone to use.

My jaw stiffened and my teeth clinched. "Bobby, the only way to avoid this is if I have your complete attention and cooperation in the classroom for the rest of this school year. Do you understand what I mean?"

Bobby continued to shift his weight, and seemed to be wondering what to do with his hands. Finally, he stuck them in his jean pockets. "Yes sir. Can we go back to the classroom now?"

I repositioned my tie, picked up my coat, and followed Bobby back into the classroom. He behaved very well for the rest of the class period.

As I talked with my colleague between classes, I explained why I needed him to sit with my class and what had taken place out behind the gym. He looked at me and said, "You do know Bobby's dad is the county sheriff, right?"

"Oops, I did not know that."

Needless to say, for the next few days I feared a visit from Bobby's dad.

He never came.

I'm sure I'll never know what happened with Bobby and his dad. Did he even tell his dad what happened? Did he tell his dad and his dad agreed with me? Those questions will remain forever unanswered.

But one thing I do know is Bobby and I underwent a transformation. He became the class sergeant at arms and took care of any students who caused problems. He became my go-to person when I needed something done. In a short period of time, Bobby transformed from the most unlovable student to a beloved friend in the classroom. When motivation occurs, we can all be transformed.

George Porter is a brother, husband, father, and grandfather who loves God. A science teacher for more than twenty years, George brings the scientific world to his presentations, Bible teaching, and writing helping his audiences embrace the God who made us all. George's calm influence on any room combined with his engaging wit will make him your favorite Phlegmatic.

Gerry Wakeland

Words To Transform Your Life

MY FATHER WAS killed just days before my fourteenth birthday. It altered my life in ways I never expected.

Suddenly a single parent left with two young girls to raise, my mother struggled dealing with her own grief and trying to help us work through ours. My younger sister had been home when our old farmhouse caught fire and was the last one to hear Daddy's voice as he shouted for her to get out of the house. I can only imagine the thoughts and feelings that were trapped inside her, much like Daddy had been trapped inside that burning house.

I had my own anguish to contend with. My world was suddenly turned upside down. So when people told me, "Deal with it and move on," I did just that. I bottled up my grief and forged ahead trying to make sense of the senseless.

As the years passed I would have fleeting memories of my daddy, memories of happier times when he took us camping or fishing or riding on Princess, our Palomino mare. I remembered the doll cradle he made for me one Christmas and how he taught me to dance the Twist when I was just ten. However with each passing year the memories grew dimmer and dimmer.

Twenty years passed by quickly and I really thought I had done what everyone had advised, "Deal with it and move on." But suddenly I was burdened by an overwhelming torment when one day I realized I could not remember my daddy ever telling me he loved me. Surely he had said those words to me as I played on his lap, followed him around in the garden, and grew into a young woman before his eyes. Why then suddenly could I not remember? I became obsessed with the thought. It haunted me night and day. I found myself frequently crying out to God asking him to please help me remember. But God remained silent.

I had been at church for a meeting and had stayed longer than planned talking to some of the women. It was late when I left to make the twenty-four-mile drive home. Strangely, I don't remember much about the drive. At one point, it seemed as if the oncoming traffic had some type of odd lights. When I reached up to rub my eyes, thinking I must be getting tired, I realized I was crying and the odd lights were because the tears made the headlights reflect like prisms.

I'm not sure how I made it to my exit that night but I do remember taking the exit. As I came to a stop at the traffic light I lost all track of time. Tears were flowing down my cheeks and my heart ached. "Please God," I begged. "I need to know my daddy loved me."

It was eerily silent when I heard the voice just as clear as if someone was sitting in the car next to me. "I am your Father and I love you and that's all that matters." I have no idea how long I sat there as the traffic light changed from red to green and back to red, over and over again. All I know is my once breaking heart was at peace.

My Father loved me. It no longer mattered if I could not remember those words of endearment coming from the lips of my earthly father. My Heavenly Father loved me and that was all I needed to hear.

Another twenty years have passed and I still look back every now and then and cherish the memories of camping and fishing with my dad. I think about the Christmases when he hung icicles on the tree one by one and made the eggnog. He made the very best eggnog.

But now I have new memories, memories made with my Heavenly Father. Memories of sitting and watching the ocean together, of long conversations as we drive across the beautiful countryside He created for my pleasure, and of the many ways He has cared and provided for me over the years.

My life was changed the day my daddy was killed; my life was transformed the day I heard Jesus say, "I love you."

Gerry Wakeland is the President and CEO of CLASSEMINARS, Inc. She loves helping Christian communicators recognize their passions, clarify their visions, and define their missions so they can articulate God's message effectively. Gerry is the mother of two grown daughters and three precious grandsons and resides in the land of enchantment, Albuquerque, New Mexico. www. classeminars.org

Edna Ellison

Pick up Your Bed and Walk

SHE'S THE ONE who got in trouble. You know, the one who had a baby in prison."

"I don't want an ex-con in my house," Joan said. "She might steal something."

I listened as the women in our Beautiful Hat Society talked about the new girl, whispering the word "trouble" as if she was spitting out a bitter vitamin.

"She even looks like trouble," Dolly said. Her words hung in the air as Heather came in with Jane, a tall young woman with her hair plastered to her scalp like spaghetti stuck to a thin tin pan. Her eyes scanned her own shoes as Heather introduced her. Jane slid into a seat near the door. I looked around at the group. The BHS loved everybody; the group's mission statement said so. These women really cared about the younger women in the church. They welcomed Sara, Carol Ann's daughter; and young Susan, the college kid; and Germaine, the new banker's wife with the blood-red lipstick—and even Timekala with the frizzy hair. They really did love everybody.

Really.

Heather started the meeting, so the whispering stopped and the Beautiful Hat Society spent the next hour talking about church donations to the poor and collecting caps before winter. After the discussion was over, I hung around, waiting to speak to Jane.

"There you are!" said Heather, walking toward me. "I think you're the perfect one!"

"For what?"

"The perfect one to take Jane to the Regional Single's Retreat at the center this year. You are going, aren't you?"

"Yes, I'd thought I would."

"I'll bet Jane would like to go." I was trapped.

I talked to Jane about the details of the retreat. Yes, she could go even though she didn't have a job yet, and she had no reserve funds to pay the conference fee. No problem. Our church had

76

a benevolence fund to cover such situations. I told her what to bring: casual clothes, walking shoes, the usual toiletries, a flashlight, and an extra pillow if she needed one. Before I knew it, I was signed up and scheduled as her reluctant roommate.

Since I was hesitant about taking a felon as a roommate—and a little ashamed before God because of my hesitancy—I knew we needed to get acquainted. The next day I picked her up for lunch. I opened the conversation by asking if she had talked to our pastor lately. She said he had counseled her the week before. He had read the story of the lame man Jesus healed and told her she should do as the lame man: pick up her bed and walk. She and I agreed about the pastor's good advice.

"I have a hard time doing that," she said. "I feel a lot of regret. It's hard to forget the past and be suddenly successful. I guess I'll keep trying. Some days I walk, and some days I just go back to bed."

When I picked her up for the retreat, Jane brought her clothes in a paper bag. She also carried an extra blanket and the big pillow she usually slept on.

"Hey, Edna!" She yelled from her driveway. "Look at me. I've picked up my bed and walked!"

We drove to the retreat, where she met many friends, some of whom had experienced similar heartbreak to hers.

A few days passed and I called Jane. "I've been crying for three days," she said. "God's been cleaning out my heart. I want to come to church with you Sunday, okay?"

From that moment on, I have loved Jane. She has become a good friend. Just last week she told me, "Edna, I'm different." I thought she was losing faith because she was not like the good Christians at my church.

"Jane, all of us are different. We just love each other in spite of our differences."

"No, I mean, ever since I picked up my bed and walked, something has changed inside me. Way down deep. I'm different here… in my heart. I feel peace for the first time."

I grinned. "I'm different too, Jane."

And I am.

Edna Ellison, known as the "Christian mentoring guru," leads a women's group called The Beautiful Hat Society—a group which doesn't wear hats. She has changed the names in this true story. From Spartanburg, South Carolina, Dr. Ellison (www.ednaellison.com) enjoys speaking at women's retreats.

Lessie Harvey

The Change in Me

THERE WERE TEN of us in the room, yet my relative singled me out for a tongue-lashing. *Why me again?*

Over the years I had learned to hold my tongue. I'd never given a tongue-lashing to any of my high school students, but occasionally I did take out my temper on others.

When an elderly cleaning woman asked me if I'd given my child to God, without hesitation I over-reacted and replied, "Are you crazy? God can't take care of me. Why would I give Him my child? I brought me to this point, not Him. He hasn't done anything for me. No, I'm not giving God my child!"

"I gave my first-born to God, and now he's a preacher," she said.

"That may be good for you, but not for me. I'm not giving my child to God!"

My friend cleaned my room in silence. Even though I spoke to her harshly, I didn't apologize. Her words haunted me. I couldn't get them out of my mind. If my tongue-lashing relative represented God, I didn't want any part of Him or her. No, I wasn't about to entrust my child to God.

Even though I had made my decision, peace escaped me. My friend's words haunted me. I couldn't get them out of my mind. Never before had I thought about God or giving my child to Him. How could I be wrestling with Him for the control of my unborn child? It didn't make sense to me.

Like my tongue-lashing relative, God wouldn't leave me alone. He wasn't nagging any of my friends. *Why me?* Because I couldn't win the battle of wills, I surrendered. If God wanted my child that badly, He could have him! To my surprise, I had peace again.

When I became pregnant with my second and third child, I immediately gave them to God, even though I never gave myself to Him. About three months after the birth of my third child, God began drawing me to Himself. I responded.

The Change in Me

I'd heard God had a sense of humor. I just couldn't figure out what he thought was funny about my insensitive relative coming for a visit. God I liked. Her I didn't. I wanted her to know the God I served. Maybe that would change her. No matter how I served her during her visits to my home, she never changed, but I changed.

Her critical and insulting words became less hurtful and offensive. I guess it was during this time that God healed my emotional wounds. I can't say when or how it happened. I just know that her words no longer cut deeply into my heart. I wasn't oozing anger and bitterness, nor was I resentful anymore. Instead of hating her and wondering why she was still alive, I thank God for giving her time to repent and turn to Him. Is my relationship with her a vibrant one? No, but it's a thousand times better than it was.

I agree with Romans 12:2, "Do not conform to the pattern of this world but be transformed by the renewing of your mind." Not only did God change my heart, he changed my mind when I trusted, believed, and obeyed Him even when I didn't see the results I desired. As long as my heart and mind are in agreement with God and His Word, I look forward to the growth and healing transformation brings in my life.

Lessie Harvey is a CLASS faculty member, writer, speaker, and Certified Christian Life Coach living in Maryland. Lessie is the author of *Becoming God's Vessel of Honor*. Her desire is to encourage, empower, and equip others to fulfill God's calling for their lives.

David W. Cary

A Dramatic Day

AS A CHILD, I dreaded the day my parents would die.

After a year of seminary in Jackson, Mississippi, my wife and I decided a family vacation was in order. My mother had experienced a stroke two years earlier so we decided to spend some time with her and Dad. We firmed up the plans, and soon we were traveling north to the beautiful Black Hills of South Dakota.

My mother loved the out-of-doors. Even though the stroke had paralyzed her left side, she had the capacity to enjoy life. As plans developed for the week, we decided to have a picnic in our back yard and invite my mother's sister and her family.

The day seemed perfect for a picnic with lots of sunshine and blue sky. We enjoyed our usual menu of hamburgers, hot dogs, baked beans, chips, and our favorite potato salad with extra onions. We stayed outside in the fresh air as long as we could, visiting and laughing. My mother loved to laugh, and this day, the family time seemed extra special. Late in the afternoon some clouds began to gather, so we started cleaning up.

My cousin needed to leave early so I walked him out to his car in the front driveway. We stood chatting for a few moments, making the most of the chance to catch up. As he inserted the key in the ignition, my aunt called from the front door, "David, your mother has suddenly become ill!" Her voice was urgent.

My aunt is a nurse, and I knew if she showed concern, something had to be wrong.

I hurried inside.

"What is happening?" I asked. I could hear my father talking to someone on the phone. My aunt was pacing the floor.

"Well, we had just wheeled her inside when she started acting sickly."

"Where is Mom now?" I managed.

"Your father and I have put her in bed."

80

A Dramatic Day

I rushed to my mother's bedside. She was lying on her right side—her good side. I sat down on the edge of the bed and put my hand on her shoulder. She slowly turned her head toward me. I could see worry on her face. "I think I am dying, and I'm a little bit afraid." Her voice was weak and shaking.

I wanted to offer some reassurance, but I was gripped with fear. What could I say? I said a quick little prayer and then heard myself saying. "Mom, you raised us kids on the Scriptures. I've heard you quote from Psalm 23 many times. 'Yea, though I walk through the valley of the shadow of death, I will fear no evil for thou art with me.'"

Her eyes were focused on mine. Then, as a look of peace filled her gaze, she smiled, reached over, and patted my hand. It was as if her faith took hold and she had overcome her fear. Moments later she slipped into unconsciousness, never to speak again.

Outside it began to storm. There were flashes of lightning, booming thunder, and torrents of rain. Soon the paramedics arrived. They took her vitals, put her on a gurney, and sped off towards the hospital. My mother appeared to be dying of a major stroke.

I stepped over to our front door and looked out at the storm. My father and aunt had gone with the ambulance. I felt very alone. I needed some comfort. *God, where are you?* I almost cried it out loud.

At that moment, the clouds parted slightly and a light patch of blue sky emerged. In my spirit, I clearly heard a response. *I'm right here—right where I've always been and always will be!*

Something began to change in me. Calmness permeated my own emotions. I began to trust the Scripture myself. God knew what He was doing and would help us all through this ordeal.

From that dramatic day, life took on a new feel. The Scriptures have become more meaningful, having greater influence on my life. As there have been many more tough times, I've had to rely on more Scriptures. Seldom have I questioned the Lord's presence. The Scriptures helped my mother while dying, and they have continued to change my life for the better while living.

David W. Cary has experience in business, ministry, and psychotherapy. He has a Bachelor of Arts degree from Kansas City College and Bible School. He has served in various roles in ministry including pastor, district superintendent, writer, and radio speaker. David and his wife Holley live in Bartlett, Tennessee.

Linda B. Correa

A Secret Place

THE CATERPILLAR, WARMLY nestled in its secret place, is unaware of metamorphosis, as wings are intricately knit together in a beautiful mosaic of unique shape and vibrant color. Nor is it aware of the new identity evolving through each stage of change.

Like a caterpillar in a cocoon, we are not aware of our transformation as it occurs.

Roused from sleep, the caterpillar is beckoned forth from this dark place. What was once a safe and necessary abode would become a grave should the worm remain in the cocoon. Struggling through walls once a haven, the caterpillar fights for life and freedom, finding strength as it pushes through its weakness. What was once ugly and mundane transforms into a new, extraordinary creature. A new world awaits its entrance with great anticipation as it bursts forth into the sun's warm embrace.

As I prepared for a trip to New Mexico, one of the many tasks on my to-do list was getting new contact lenses. As I sat in the ophthalmologist's chair, I slipped my glasses back onto my face and looked up. "You look like a completely different person with your glasses on," she said. "You look completely transformed."

I smiled as I thought of my own journey. Her statement took me back to my teen years to a dark-skinned, lanky girl with frizzy hair and glasses that were too big for her young face. Most of my life was spent in two different worlds. One was my inner world of darkness and emotional turmoil. Every day was a struggle to survive and an ongoing battle to find my identity—my own cocoon. The other was my outer world, where the art of make-up and great sense of fashion came naturally to me. I became a chameleon of sorts, with the ability to change my appearance with the wave of a brush.

I learned early-on how the power of transformation is a tool that could be used to hide away from the world. My life became a stage and each day a performance, however my deepest desire was to change inwardly. I wanted with all of my heart to be real and to be able to smile without crying on the inside. Then I met Jesus. Years passed as He gently set the broken pieces of my heart in their proper place. Little by little, I began to notice differences in myself. The true evidence came when those around me began to see the same changes I did. No longer on a stage so to speak, my life's course took a turn. I began to live for an audience of One.

As God took me through each stage of healing I realized I was transformed. I was being knit back together in a secret place. My wounds were being healed, my voice restored, and a new song placed in my heart that emanated beautiful shades of vibrant color. I became renewed, I was alive and a new-found hope filled my soul. I was beckoned by a familiar voice on the other side of the frail walls that encompassed me. As I found myself stirring from my deep slumber, I struggled, but this time for my life. The more I pushed the stronger I became. Suddenly, the warm light of the Son broke through my dark cocoon. This haven, once a safe place, could no longer hold me. My new world awaited with great anticipation as a new creature made her entrance. I came forth unsure and unstable but then, I spread my wings. And as I pushed off carefree, the soft wind caught me and I soared. I took the chance offered to me and did what I was compelled to do, what I was created to do—fly.

A passionate, inspirational speaker, Linda Correa delves deeply into matters of the heart. She is a prayer warrior, Bible study teacher, mother of two, and first-time grandmother. Linda is currently writing her first manuscript, a book about hope and healing following sexual abuse.

Audrey Chevalier

Prayer Moves the Mountains

PRAYER. IT IS a powerful thing. But what does it really mean to pray? Well, the exact definition is a form of religious practice meant to activate volitional rapport. Surely, it means something more. I think it means to communicate with God, in His presence, and that is not something I used to do very much.

When we moved, I was not a happy camper. I retreated into my own little box of sadness. I didn't talk much to anyone, especially God.

My parents talked to me and found out I was struggling. At first, I just didn't want to do it. I preferred my own little box, thank you very much. I was perfectly fine on my own, or so I thought. Months went by, and I needed God more and more. One day I reached my limit. I needed help, so I decided to ask for it, but this time from God.

Gradually, I became more open with God. I talked to Him, asked for things, or said a little, "Hi God! How's it going?" Praying more has really changed me. I am more stable emotionally and spiritually. Prayer has drawn me closer to God, and I have used it in many difficult situations.

One time, I had to pray for God's help when I was going to a volleyball tournament. I was riding with Mrs. Samuels and her kids, Olivia and Ivy. They each played volleyball too, so it was really important that we got there on time. When we were close, we got lost. The roads were so confusing. Mrs. Samuels was literally crying out to God. Then she asked me to pray for help. So I did. I asked Him to give her the wisdom to know where to go, and we figured it out. Although we were a little late, I have a wonderful coach, who is always willing to forgive.

Another time, we went to Arizona. We had to drive for two days squished in a cramped little car. I prayed for patience. It was a long trip from Houston to Phoenix. Our grandparents had bought each of us an iPod Touch, but when those things ran out of battery, uh-oh, look out! Of course, that's where my praying skills came in. When my sister said something that was annoying, I would pray, "Please God, help me. Give me a little patience, because I don't want to hurt my sister's feelings."

Praying is also a great way to get to know your Father in heaven. By simply talking to him, you can find out how loving your Creator really is. God is eager for you to know Him, and it's really not that hard. It's simple. All you have to do is say, "Hi, Lord. Would you show me what to do today?" That's all it takes. Honestly.

Learning to pray and to be open with God has transformed me. The Bible says to cast all your worries and cares on him. That has been a lot easier with prayer. Talking to God has really changed me. But God is not finished with me yet, so until He is, I will remain faithful in everything I do for the Lord. And I will always be transformed with prayer.

Audrey Chevalier is an 11-year-old writer from Missouri City, Texas.

A New Heart

Judi Clarke

DON'T DO THAT to me! Please don't take her from me!" There on the living room floor wedged between the couch and coffee table, I had it out with God.

My closest friend had been through so much in the last three months. Her surprise twins were four months old when she heard the diagnosis that, at age forty, she needed a heart transplant. The following weeks were terrifying for her and everyone who loved her. After dying in the night and being brought back to life, she was flown to another hospital one-hundred miles away. There, she was stabilized and endured the physical and emotional roller coaster of facing her reality. Back home, her friends and church family waited anxiously. We witnessed God's detailed care in answering prayers for her health, spirits, and specific family needs.

Still, I struggled to trust God with my dear friend's life. Always the fearful type, I knew He sometimes allows the unthinkable. Reluctant to hope, I grew encouraged by seeing how intricately He'd taken care of my friend and her family. As the weeks passed, I dared to believe the hope unfolding before me.

At last I got the call saying a heart was available her. I expressed my fears to the caller, and then quickly calmed them by saying, "After God has paved such a meticulous road pointing to her recovery, I can't believe He'd drop us off a cliff by taking her from us now."

"But you know, Judi, He still could," came the reply.

I felt like the breath had been knocked out of me. After I hung up, I fell to my knees in front of the couch. I grew angry at God, angry in advance for something He could do. I felt betrayed by the tender care He'd shown during this crisis. How could He do such a thing to us after the hope He'd given us? I couldn't bear the thought of losing my friend. My heart grew cold toward God. "If You take her from us now, after all this, I'm done with You! I'll believe You for salvation, but as for everyday life, I'm done!" It was a dark place, this imagined scenario.

A New Heart

Desperately I cried out, "Please don't do that!" I envisioned life without my friend and saw how angry I'd be at God, and how hard my heart could grow toward Him. Rocking back and forth with my face toward the ground, I sobbed into my hands and repeated the same helpless plea. Then suddenly I cried, "Don't abandon me because I need You!"

I froze, shocked to hear my silent prayer transformed. I went from being afraid of losing my friend to being afraid of losing God. I saw what life would be like if my fearful heart turned angrily away from Him. Cold. Hard. Empty and lifeless.

I realized something that day, and it changed my life. Even if God were to take my friend from this earth, He was my only hope to survive the pain. I couldn't turn my back on God; I need Him too much. I *must* trust Him with the pain He allows in my life. That day I prayed for the first time like Job, saying, "…though He slay me, yet will I trust Him" (Job 13:15 NIV).

My friend got her new heart that day fourteen years ago and she continues to live a full life. I got a new heart that day, too. A heart that knows how much I need God and can't live without Him. In order to "have" Him, I must trust Him, even when He allows pain. I learned that even if God allows things in my life which I don't consider safe, the only hope to get through them is with Him, trusting Him. His presence became far more security to me than the safe, pain-free life I'd spent years longing for. I see now that trusting Him in all things is the only safe place to live.

Judi Clarke lives with her husband in Arizona in an off-grid cabin they built with their own hands. She chronicles their country life on her blog, www.25acres.blogspot.com. Judi also helps others move from fear to a deep and trusting relationship with God through her blog www.fear2eternity.blogspot.com.

Anita Davis Yates

A Teacher Transformed

THE LITTLE, SOILED face looked up at me as I grabbed her backpack. She had taken things from our classroom and was headed toward the bus.

"What's in that backpack? How could you take this? These things don't belong to you!" She looked up at me, fear evident in her eyes, but she said nothing.

Although I didn't punish her, my harsh tone and the volume of my voice frightened this child. Later, I regretted my words.

When I first began teaching, I thought I knew everything there was to know about young children. At the time, I had no children of my own, but when my son was born my perspective changed. I looked at him and marveled at every physical feature. Even hints of a strong will and personality as he developed were precious to me. My love for this little human being was amazing to me. In experiencing this love for my son, I began to understand a fraction of God's love for us and his command for us to love others in like manner. If I loved my son this much, didn't other parents feel the same?

With these insights, my teaching changed. Now, I see how important each child is in God's sight, to their parents, and to me. I've become more sensitive, more loving, and more forgiving of these little children. I've worked on balancing my desire to teach right and wrong with loving each child in their current level of learning and their family situation. I always want them to feel valued and loved.

Looking back, I can see how I am like a little child to God. I realize He has been sensitive to my shortcomings. Although I often disappoint Him, He shows great compassion, love, and forgiveness. When I fail, He confronts me, but also restores me. This restoration allows me to continue the journey of conforming and transforming.

The day I confronted my young classroom thief, I failed to restore her. She made an error, which needed correction, but she also needed to know she was forgiven and still important and valuable to me. She needed to know everyone makes mistakes and every mistake is a learning experience.

Sometimes, teachers who take a stricter approach to discipline criticize me for being too lenient. But when appropriate, I pass on what I learned to other teachers who struggle with student misbehavior. I explain the way we confront and handle misbehavior is key to helping students understand that while their choice of action was inappropriate, they are still loved. Just as I am still becoming the person God desires for me to be, so these children are learning and changing.

Anita Davis Yates lives in beautiful East Tennessee with husband, Rod, two horses, a dog, cat, and twelve fish. She is an elementary school teacher and is in business with her husband. Anita enjoys weaving spiritual application into stories of her teaching experiences.

Depression Busters

BY MID-LIFE, I expected a fair amount of stability. I didn't expect to discover that my dad is not my biological father.

The first few weeks I grieved. "God, I know You're my Father, but I need to *feel* Your arms around me. Show me how to survive this news. What is the purpose?"

Each morning, I woke to the smog of depression. Sometimes taking a shower required more energy than I could muster. When I wasn't looking at my face, fingers, and toes, I was thinking about them. Did they resemble *his*? My biological father's?

And then, on December 4, 2010, an epiphany struck. If it takes twenty-one days to change a habit, what would happen if I spent twenty-one days trying to overcome depression?

I went online, researched natural sources of melancholy relief, and wrote my findings in my journal. The next day, I wrote the first Depression Buster (a set of focal points, designed to help overcome despair) on my Facebook® note page.

When waves of discouragement threatened to drown me, I'd read and resolve to follow the Depression Buster steps.

On the second day, I followed the same pattern.

- Write a short story to express my emotions.
- Research proven natural remedies to help the physical aspects of depression.
- Find a mental exercise or positive reinforcement to reframe my outlook.
- Search the Bible for a passage that spoke healing to my dilemma.
- Document the findings. I knew from experience that writing anything down helps to reinforce it in my mind.

Depression Busters

On the third day, private messages from Facebook® friends who'd read the Depression Busters flooded my inbox. People in crisis, who were fighting suicidal thoughts or whose relationships were falling apart. The stories were varied, but the message was the same. "Please keep writing. Your stories are helping me cope with my own problems. I'm desperate for answers."

As I continued researching and writing, I learned tears are your body's release valve for stress, sadness, grief, anxiety, and frustration. Tears heal and detoxify. Water elevates our mood. Cleaning up the clutter in a corner of a room offers a sense of accomplishment when a whole room is too much to handle. Resolve can change everything.

Days turned into weeks, and one Depression Buster connected to another. Many people continued to share their struggles with me, while God remodeled my life. By allowing me to help others, God helped me.

It only takes twenty-one days to change a habit.

My situation hadn't changed. I still had emotions to process, questions to answer, and reality to face. I may never know the man who fathered me, but I know my *real* Father. I look like Him. He created my face, fingers, and toes. They resemble His.

At the end of twenty-one days, Christmas morning dawned bright and clear. Snow sparkled in the sun like the white lights on our tree. A string of beats pumped through my veins in joyful anticipation. I lay in bed and thought about Christmases past and the one in my present. I ripped the paper off my favorite gift with child-like joy. I was despair-free.

Many human beings suffer with depression, but with God's help we can get through it. Through Jesus Christ, we are transformed. Through us, He sometimes helps others. Through the hard times, we begin to look like Him. Transformation is a process of being renewed, one day at a time.

> "And we all, who with unveiled faces contemplate the Lord's glory, are being transformed into his image with ever-increasing glory, which comes from the Lord, who is the Spirit."
> —2 Corinthians 3:18 NIV

Anita Agers-Brooks is a Communications Specialist, Certified Personality Trainer, Christian speaker, and writer. She and her husband Ricky live in Missouri. Contact her via www.freshstartfreshfaith.org

Mikelyn Bolden

The Ring Master

I LOOKED DOWN at my hand and noticed the two wedding bands were missing. I was standing in the middle of a grand Tennessee plantation on my baby sister's wedding day.

Although thrilled to serve as her maid of honor, I also felt skeptical of how her spontaneous spirit and planner personality would mesh during the wedding process. The week of the wedding I found myself doing all the things a good maid of honor should, including stuffing gift bags for hotel guests, taking the bride for a pedicure, buying fifty pounds of powdered sugar for the cake, throwing a last minute bachelorette party, and, of course, giving a rehearsal dinner speech.

On the day of the wedding my sister and future brother-in-law asked me to be in charge of holding the rings, saying, "We know you're the responsible one."

As the bridal party paraded onto the lawn, I slipped the rings on my fingers then gathered mine and my sister's bouquets. For some reason, I still don't fully understand, my sister, despite her tomboy style, chose a dress with an elaborate train. My job was to fluff the train at each photo stop. On the third fluff, I looked down at my fingers and gasped. The rings were missing.

With my heart in my throat, I scanned the ground. The two love birds remained unaware as I whispered to a nearby groomsmen and bridesmaid, "I lost the rings."

Expecting an I-can't-believe-you-did-that reply, instead, I heard, "Okay, God you know where these rings are. Help us find these rings."

They continued praying aloud as we searched the ground. I tried to remember where we had stopped and the last time I had seen the rings, all the while hearing booming self-accusations, *How could you let this happen? You're so irresponsible. You've ruined the whole wedding. Everyone thinks you're stupid.*

"You lost the rings?" said a bridesmaid, loud enough for everyone nearby to hear.

I turned red and my whole body began to shake. I couldn't continue the search. All bridesmaids, groomsmen, kids, decorators, extended family members, and photographers bent, searching the grass, determined to find the rings. Rather than casting me condescending glances, they smiled and said, "We'll find them." I was shocked as I watched these people focus on the answer rather than the problem.

I found the laidback, free-spirited bride and groom nestled against a large oak tree, unruffled by the turn of events. I sobbed and blubbered my apologies as I approached. "You said I was the responsible one and I lost the rings. I'll pay for them. I'm sure you hate me. I'm so sorry."

My sister cupped her hands around my wet face, looked me straight in the eyes, and said, "You are more important to me than these rings. We love you. You are more important than just things."

Those three sentences transformed my life. I realized that if any object becomes more important to me than the person standing in front of me, I'm devaluing what God values most.

The groom wiped my eyes with his handkerchief as the moment was interrupted by a host of cheers. With the help of a metal detector, the search committee had found the missing rings. As I looked back at the wedding couple, I realized that even if the rings hadn't been found, I had experienced the true meaning of grace.

Mikelyn Bolden is a young adult fantasy fiction writer and journalist. She has also led many inner city humanitarian projects around the world which inspired a passion to mentor the younger generations. She lives with her husband in Dothan, Alabama.

Robert Enns

Transformation
Dissolves Tensions

JASON WAS A Canadian newcomer to Bangladesh. He wanted to find someone who could help him straighten out the conflicting impressions which he had been receiving in his first few days in Bangladesh.

However, the angry shouts of the demonstrators marching down the street rang in his ears. "Bideshishomoshabidhaiditayhobay!" ("We must get rid of foreign problems!").

Why do the crowds blame foreigners for their problems? he wondered, as he neared the office of an organization he had heard about. Jason wished the police or army would come and shut these young demonstrators down with whatever force necessary, even if that seemed harsh. *For the police at least, the end would justify the means,* he thought.

As he looked at the sign in front of the office, Jason mused that the organization's name seemed rather unusual. FACT (Facilitating Active Community Transformation) seemed to be a strange name, so he was curious to find out more.

When Jason entered the front room of the office, the receptionist greeted him, asked his name, and then took him to a room where some people were meeting. They welcomed him, invited him to take a seat at the table, and immediately returned to a very active discussion. They were discussing ways they could possibly persuade the demonstrators to stop their demonstrations, which had lasted three days now. One person mentioned that he knew one of the prime organizers of the demonstrations. Jason thought, *Oh good, that should help them shut those young punks down! If they back the organizers into a corner, those guys will come to their senses pretty quickly. I'll help tell the police, if necessary.*

But when Jason heard what the people in this room were saying, he was puzzled. They were discussing a verse in the Bible which says "be transformed by the renewing of your minds, so that you may be able to determine what God's will is – what is proper, pleasing, and perfect."

Each person around the table suggested how this approach could help reconcile the differences among the people who were demonstrating and the people at whom they were shouting.

Jason was puzzled as he looked around the room. Judging by the people's clothing, some certainly did not look like Christians. "Pardon me for asking," Jason interrupted, "but is this a Christian organization?"

"Yes, it definitely is," replied a young man. "We work together as an organization based on Christian values and we often study biblical passages for guidance on how best to address difficult situations."

"But we as staff are not all Christians," added a young woman, who had a scarf over her hair. "In fact, the largest number of us are Muslims, along with quite a few Hindus and Buddhists, together with Christians. We all appreciate the goals, programs, and impact of FACT, and we agree to being guided by the Christian values which this organization is based on."

"Doesn't that lead to disagreements?" Jason asked.

"Not really," responded an older man. "We each have different perspectives, but we also each contribute a better understanding of our own ethnic and religious background. That helps the team determine the appropriate ways of addressing problems we encounter in our work and in society. Yes, we do have disagreements and tensions, sometimes. But usually, the teamwork goes fairly well."

"Take those demonstrators, for example," another woman added. "Some of them are just frustrated they haven't been able to get jobs yet. Some of them get caught up in the mood of an angry crowd. But some of them have legitimate concerns which need to be dealt with. We want to assure them there are people, those of us in FACT, who are willing to listen to them and work with them to find long-term solutions."

"Just like that verse says," continued the older man. "Transformation to renew our minds, so that we can work together for the kind of peaceful and constructive solution that God wants."

As Jason reflected on this, he realized this was completely the reverse of what he had been thinking when he walked into this office; but it made a lot of sense now. He was glad he had witnessed this meeting and he was keen to hear more.

The names in this story have been changed.

Rob Enns has worked in international development programs in many countries, with both Christian and secular organizations. He enjoys working together with people of different backgrounds and perspectives, to enhance cooperation and community development. When Christian values form the basis of that cooperation, the long-term impact is even greater. www.building-effective-sustainable-teams.com

John Gilden

Transformation of a Scout

JIMMY SLUMPED ON the floor, trying desperately to melt into the small gathering of local Boy Scouts. This was his first meeting and he wasn't thrilled. His mom suggested he join the local troop but looking around the room of experienced tenderfoot, second, and first class boy scouts, he wondered if this was a bad idea. As the boys finished reciting the scout oath, Jimmy folded his arms and plopped back down. Who would have thought one day this frustrated young man would transform into a leader?

There's nothing quite like the Boy Scouts of America to transform such boys as Jimmy into a generation of responsible men, ready to take on life's challenges. I should know, for more than twenty years I've witnessed countless boys transform from children to responsible, young adults. Beginning with the first campout these boys have responsibility thrust upon them that other boys their age do not experience until much later in the life, if ever.

I recall in Jimmy's early scout experience when he began to lose complete interest in the whole idea. His attitude grew worse. Jimmy's mom expressed her concern with his behavior, not only in Scouts but at home. At this point we decided he needed encouragement to help him realize his potential. We could see the leadership qualities that Jimmy wasted. So one night after the meeting we took him aside and told him of our concern. We could see the talent God had given him to truly lead others. We watched him on several campouts where other boys gravitated to him and he needed to make a choice; was he going to lead them in the right or wrong direction?

So the next outing we challenged him to take the lead. He would take responsibility for all patrol activities including cooking and cleaning. Jimmy doubted his ability to rise to the occasion, but reluctantly accepted our challenge. We encouraged him and explained we would be close by to help him with the task if needed. Jimmy did fine on the campout and in the next few weeks, we began to see a change in his attitude. There was an excitement about being at the meetings.

He began to take on more responsibility, even approaching the leaders to determine if there were other things he could help with. We gladly gave Jimmy additional responsibilities in the troop. As he progressed in rank, I had the opportunity to praise him in front of the troop. There were other times when I was able to praise Jimmy for a good job in front of his mother.

One night Jimmy's mom asked to speak with me. She wanted me to know that his attitude at home had changed for the better. He did his chores without being told and no longer talked back. She was amazed at the "new" Jimmy and wanted us to know how thankful she was to the Scout leaders for the encouragement and help we had given in turning him around.

It has been interesting to observe the transformation of Jimmy from someone on the wrong path, headed for trouble, into a boy leader in the troop. Jimmy is not through with his scouting career. He mentioned to me that he has set his goal to earn his Eagle Scout rank, the highest award a boy can earn in scouting.

As Christians, we are often like Jimmy. Sometimes we need an "attitude adjustment." God waits to transform us; all we need to do is ask. Like Jimmy, we all need encouragement. This can come from reading the Bible, listening to a sermon, or from a conversation with a good friend. God wants us as men to be the leaders in our home, in our communities, and in our church. He wants us to stand up and be bold (Joshua 1:9). Are you up to the challenge?

John Gilden has been involved as a Scout leader with Cub Scouts, Weebelo Scouts, and Boy Scouts since 1991. John has served as Scoutmaster of Troop 5 in Spartanburg, South Carolina, for twelve years. He has encouraged many boys to set and achieve the goal of Eagle Scout.

Elise Schneider

Trio Transformation

IF WE LIVE long enough, none of us will make it through life without battle scars. Any thorns in your life? Devastated by the death of someone you love? Disillusioned by betrayal? I have experienced and survived all of these. But my most piercing thorn of all was my divorce.

Dear Lord how can I possibly live through divorce from the love of my life? I thought my self-esteem had been shredded. I was the first divorcee in my family. Each time I looked into the mirror, I imagined an invisible scarlet "D" for divorcee on my clothing.

As I fought self-pity, I repeatedly dropped to my knees and cried out to God. "Lord, I've clung to Your promises in the Bible all my life. Please help!"

One afternoon the familiar words of Romans 8:28 surfaced, "And we know that in all things God works for the good of those who love him, who have been called according to his purpose" (NIV).

"But how can *good* possibly come from this miserable divorce?" I demanded. As I argued with God, a quotation my son had sent me from Charles Swindoll's essay, "Attitude," captured my thoughts.

"The longer I live, the more I realize the impact of attitude…. The remarkable thing is we have a choice every day regarding the attitude we will embrace…. I am convinced that life is ten percent what happens to me and ninety percent how I react to it…. And so it is with you."

I sighed, "Yes, Lord, You have given me choices. I can choose to wallow in self-pity or I can allow you to transform my attitude."

Then I remembered a class my church had been advertising. I arose from my kneeling position and dressed quickly in an outfit I realized no longer had the invisible scarlet "D." Within a few minutes I enrolled in a year-long outreach class.

Each Wednesday evening my classmates and I met for instruction on sharing our Christian faith by establishing relationships and trust with those we would meet; praying before, during,

98

and after our meetings; and witnessing about our Lord while leaving the results to the Holy Spirit. Prior to each class, appointments had been made with church visitors who stated they would welcome more information. Each class participant and a partner traveled to our assigned home to meet with the appointees. Linda, my partner, and I took turns presenting our faith.

Week after week, I experienced a return of peace and restored excitement about my life. Because of the class, I was awed God might use me in some mighty way.

Please, Lord, help me introduce You to others became my constant prayer.

The opportunity came the next Wednesday night. Sandy, a lovely new bride, answered our knock and welcomed us. Linda and I thanked her for allowing us to visit and admired a beautiful seascape painting above the fireplace. It was Linda's turn to lead the witnessing process. As I relaxed in a comfortable corner chair to observe, a young man approached with another chair in tow.

"I'm Sandy's husband; she and I have the same first name." he said.

Before I could respond, he began to fire biblical questions my way. "Do you believe this stuff? Does God really answer prayer?"

I realized that even though I was not the presenter, I had this unexpected opportunity to witness. "Yes, to both your questions, Sandy," I said. "I've believed in God and the Bible since I was six-years-old. And He always answers our prayers. Sometimes it's not the answer we want, but He knows what is best for us."

I let him think for a moment. Then I asked "Would you like to accept Jesus into your life?"

To my amazement, he said, "Yes!"

That night both husband and wife accepted Him as Savior. When they announced the decision to each other, they hugged with joy. As I watched, the final traces of self pity vanished. My life, like theirs, was transformed forever. Truly, it was a trio transformation night!

Dr. Elise Douglass Schneider serves on the CLASS Advisory Board and is an international speaker and author. Her many publications include contributions to *Guideposts* and *Focus on the Family*®. Elise's career spanned thirty plus years, including two community college presidencies. She lives in Port Hueneme, California. www.eliseschneider.com; elisedschneider@gmail.com

Myrna Parks

From Desperate To Delivered

ILIKE TO tell people about growing up on a small farm in western Kentucky surrounded by blue skies and butterflies. On one side of my house, about a mile down the road was the schoolhouse where I learned reading, writing, and a little arithmetic. On the other side of my house, just beyond a field of tall green corn, was the tiny country church where I learned about Jesus.

There were no theologians in our congregation. Only a few members who could not read or write and some who said, "cheer" instead of "chair." These were simple country folks with calloused hands and tender hearts who loved the Lord and taught me about the Savior who died on the cross for my sins.

Christ was always a part of my life. Some children have imaginary friends, but for me there was no need. I had Jesus. I walked with Him and talked with Him. By the time I was ten years old, I had made a public profession of faith and was baptized into the fellowship of believers. My life should have been good; it should have been easy.

Less than one month after my seventeenth birthday, I married my husband. I had a five-month-old daughter from a previous marriage. Although my husband is fourteen years older than me and we have now been married thirty-nine years, my life has not been easy.

For years, I wandered in and out of the desert of despair. One day, I came to the end. I could not take another step without help.

Eleven years ago, I came home from work, walked past my husband who was stretched out in his favorite recliner. I went into my bedroom and locked the door. Retrieving an old-fashioned handgun from the closet, I released the safety on the loaded pistol, backed myself against the wall, and with the gun pressed to my chest, I begged the Lord to let me die!

I cried out!

The Lord heard my plea.

Within a few hours I found myself confined inside a hospital with bars on the windows and locks on the doors. I quickly realized when God takes over, nothing else matters.

There were all kinds of people in that facility. There were drug addicts and alcoholics. There were secretaries and housewives. There was a young woman who was bulimic, an old woman who self-mutilated, prostitutes, and professional people. But all of us had one thing in common. We could not take another step without help.

Not instantly but miraculously, God reached down and lifted me out of the pit of depression. Although I had never stopped trusting the Lord for the hereafter, somewhere along life's painful pathway, I had ceased to trust Him for the here and now.

I am glad Jesus never leaves us. Regardless of our circumstances, He never forsakes us. Many patients inside that facility had been there before, and I suspected would be back again. But when I left there ten days later, I knew in my heart I would never return.

In His time and according to His plan, the Lord placed my feet firmly, once again, upon His path. He birthed a passion in my heart to see believers set free from the lies of the enemy.

Now, I am writing, teaching women, and leading Bible studies. I remind believers of the new song and message the Lord has given us: we are bought with a price, we are sealed with His covenant, and we are the bride of the King!

Myrna Parks is active in women's ministry and empathizes with the challenges women face while juggling career and family. Her heart is to see women experience peace in a world of turmoil. This story gives a glimpse into how Myrna discovered true peace. For more information visit Myrna's website at www.straighttalkcleanwalk.com.

Shona Neff

Water and Wait

ONE SUMMER I dreamed of transforming the long-neglected patch by my front porch into a beautiful oasis of green. After much thought, I skipped home from the nursery with three cute, narrow-leafed plants splashed with white speckles.

After carefully digging the holes that would cradle my cherished plants, I watered and waited, watered and waited, and watered and waited some more. The warm summer days turned into weeks and then months, but nothing happened with my plants.

When summer's heat started yielding to the cooler temperatures of the approaching fall, something caught my eye as I walked by my garden: little speckled shoots of green and white were peeking up at me from all over the dismal patch of dirt. The trio of plants had been busy after all.

As I stood staring at the miracle orchestrated by an intricate system of roots, my thoughts drifted to my oldest son. From the day he was born, I dreamed of the time he would become a man. Sure, there were times it seemed like I was raising a barbarian. I wondered if he would ever emerge from the awkward teen years. My husband and I modeled the Christian life as best we could, but many seasons came and went when our son showed no spiritual growth. But, we watered and waited, watered and waited, and watered and waited some more. The "watering" consisted of prayers flooding the throne room of heaven. We also nourished the growing child on the words of wisdom flowing like a river from the Bible straight into the mind and spirit of a seeker. We watered and waited.

Thank goodness the rain from heaven continually washed over our family allowing my husband and me to set a good example for our ever-watching son. There were times when he looked like those speckled little plants sitting, doing nothing. We wondered if he was ever going to reach the potential God tucked into his soul before the foundation of time. We watered and waited. Time seemed to crawl by like the passing of many summers.

But then the shoots of transformation peeked through. One summer my son asked, "Mom, if I get serious about God, will I have to give some things up?"

Despite being completely startled by the question I smiled. "Yes, son, you will. But, God doesn't expect you to look like a seasoned Christian on the first day you get serious about him. As you grow you will give things up for Him because you want to." That simple question was a little shoot peeking up through the dirt.

Another shoot burst forth when my son decided to read Proverbs. When he finished the book of wisdom, he sought my guidance and pursued the joy in Philippians. Another shoot of life burst forth when he confessed that his wallet was empty because he gave his last twenty dollars to a homeless man at a gas station. Compassion, a wonderful root guiding any man. What about fierce loyalty to his friends, or making sure a female friend gets home safely—more shoots creating a spiritual oasis in a dark world.

However, the explosion of spiritual growth burst forth when he faced a situation with the potential to mar his future job prospects.

After giving much thought to his predicament, he concluded that if he prayed and did everything within his power to set things right and it still affected his future, maybe God was allowing the obstacle in order to lead him down a more excellent path. In that moment, our son experienced God's transforming peace.

Thank goodness God works behind the scenes creating a miracle of transformation in each of our hearts. Not only does He work things out for our own good, but He works even when it seems nothing is happening. Firm spiritual roots often develop in the hidden places accessed only by God. When the time is right, the shoots peek through to the outside world like my green and white-specked plants, like the long-awaited revelations and actions of a beloved child.

Never underestimate the hidden power of God. The miracle of unseen roots transformed my beloved son revealing a beautiful garden in its time. Our role was to water and wait.

Shona Neff writes and speaks on inspirational topics. She has been featured in several online magazines and blogs. She helps people improve their relationships on her personality blog, www.shonaneff.com. She is at home in northern New Mexico with her husband and trio of terriers.

Cynthia Leepper

Value Added

SUCCESSFUL CAREER ACHIEVEMENTS in the private sector are often rewarded with bonus checks, promotions, and a corner office with a view. But I work in the public sector. Our rewards are increased workloads and tighter deadlines due to budget constraints. Whenever someone retires or leaves, their position remains vacant and others have to take on the additional responsibilities.

My supervisors changed five times in two years during a series of reorganizations. Leadership shuffled us around like we were pawns on a chessboard. They promoted me to management, yet my pay remained the same.

I established an excellent reputation as a project manager who can get the job done. Some of my own personal productivity solutions became templates for our organization. My project teams overcame challenges to accomplish several enterprise-level initiatives. Leadership hailed our work as a model for other teams to follow.

It was difficult to hang onto joy when I experienced intermittent meltdowns. I was exhausted, overloaded, and angry that my achievements as a manager weren't recognized and rewarded with a managerial title and pay. It just wasn't fair. I had a heavy load of responsibilities to carry. Working overtime had become habitual. I looked online and realized how underpaid I was.

It was time to escalate the issue to my supervisor. "Steve, I'd appreciate it if you'd contact decision makers to change my payroll title so I can get a raise."

"Did you return the form to Personnel?"

"I didn't know there was a form."

"Everyone should have received a form. I'll look into why you didn't get one."

Steve learned Personnel had missed me completely. My position didn't exist at our organization. I had taken on all this work, yet didn't even register with my company. Four months later, my promotion to a managerial title was finally approved.

Value Added

We lost another project manager while I waited for my raise, and my workload increased again. Feeling overworked, underpaid, and undervalued, I called my sister in Kansas City to see if my niece's expected baby had arrived.

"The baby is dying," my sister said.

Though work problems consumed me, my family took priority. I dropped everything.

I'm so grateful to God for my precious memories of "Jayse-Time." God used Jayse' brief life to touch mine with his sweet smile and attentive gaze, so fresh from God. Nobody expected Jayse to do anything, yet he was loved and valued. He taught me that whether I am respected or honored or paid doesn't add value, and that position, titles, and achievements are meaningless where family's concerned.

I had worked hard to fulfill my desire to become invaluable at my workplace. But the truth is if I were to leave there for some reason, they'd assign my responsibilities to someone else. The work would still get done.

I'm beginning to understand that I'm valued for who I am, not for what I do or don't do. I no longer find my value in my paycheck or among my coworkers. My value is in the Kingdom of God. Jayse taught me that.

Cynthia Leepper provides practical teaching that can be applied for victorious Christian living. Her passion is ministry for those who desire to experience God's presence and blessings in everyday life. Cynthia speaks and writes about faith that embraces God as a loving Father that desires to partner with His children for great adventures.

Bill Kemp

What Develops

"LET'S SEE WHAT develops," he'd say. He'd slid the paper face down into the bath. The joke was well worn from telling, but I'd nod in appreciation. The darkroom was like a magician's cave, with its muttered incantations, red glow, rhythmic movements, chemical smell, and me, age ten, his sorcerer's apprentice.

Behind us the radio hissed a Pirates' ball game. So sacred was this room's silence that my father tuned it low. The count of strikes against Clemente were whispered like a prayer. My father touched the paper twice with his tongs, ensuring that it lay entirely submerged, then gently rocked the tray. I glanced at the sweeping second hand of the clock. After exactly thirty-seconds, my father flipped the paper over and tapped it with the tongs twice. Three more times the clock hands traveled half its circle. He rocked the tray to keep the developing solution stirred.

After two minutes, the print moved to the stop bath, then to the fixer. Each motion orchestrated with a skilled hand. Father used the tongs like a wand. The few seconds when the paper lay face up in the developer, though, were the magical ones. The 8x10 was always blank when he first turned it over, then slowly an image emerged.

My older brother had a different experience with our father. For the first born, the hurdles are always higher. He also entered his age of curiosity while our father was struggling to make a go of his business. My brother knew more of our father's absence. The tools of the workplace often crept home with our father: office papers, perfectionism, and the desire to reengineer loved ones to rigid specifications. Things have a way of being passed down through families. Darkness can leave its shadows. One of our father's stories was how at age sixteen, he was given the task of building an addition onto their farmhouse. Grandfather's work was on the road. Each morning he awoke our father before dawn, detailing what was expected to be done next. In the waning evening he returned, materials for the next day upon his truck. He cast a critical eye over what had been completed. Only this much? Many days were spent redoing what had failed inspection. Youngest children have a way of ducking under expectations, but my brother received similar evening inspections. In time my brother became a lawyer and made a career of helping people to perfect their documents. Lacking such patience, I found it simpler to deal with image and metaphor.

A decade before his death, my father gave up his darkroom. I moved the enlarger and trays into my own basement. One of the items found among the miscellaneous junk was a roll of film that had never been developed. Eventually, I processed it. The results were mundane. Scenes from our backyard, taken almost forty years ago. My brother and I appear in one or two, but we are blurry. The album my mother keeps has better photographs.

I felt disappointed. Here was something I had not expected. A roll of film my father had shot badly. We sometimes go through life failing to give the grace for failure to those we love. We make an idol out of perfection. Then another thought occurred to me. Light had struck the film so many years ago, and nothing happened.

Photography is a latent process, meaning that what has been made possible in one instant is not manifested until later. The blank page is turned over in the developer and each silver crystal touched by light is changed. This is who we are. We are touched by the grace of various lights. We experience things in one moment that may not be manifested until much later.

The Apostle John describes one instant long ago when God became flesh and those touched by his light received grace upon grace. I add to this my own experience of standing as an apprentice in a dark place. While perfectionists fear the final judgment and Christ's arrival at earth's evening, I have always depended upon grace.

I wait to see what develops in me, for now, my image remains in the developer's bath. I long for the negative to become transformed into positive. Then I expect all will be surprised. The image of my life will be the face of God.

Bill Kemp has a pastor's heart and a dreamer's mind. He has published nine nonfiction books for church leaders and a variety of short fiction pieces, including chancel drama. In his not yet released novel, *Bethany's People*, Lazarus experiences Jesus' Passion. Find him at www.notperfectyet.com.

Pamela R. Watts

Transformed through Nonconformity

L IKE MOST TEENS, I was often torn between uniqueness and acceptance. It's a risky thing to embrace one's individuality, and there is comfort in following the crowd. For many years I wrestled with this contradiction. Two things I wanted to avoid at all cost: 1) blending into the crowd so well that no one noticed me and 2) moving so far from the crowd that no one could understand me. I wanted both distinction *and* approval.

A husband and two children later, God invited us to add an unconventional element to our traditional family through international adoption. With two biological children already, our decision was unexpected and raised a few eyebrows. At those times, God was quick to remind me how I had never wanted to look "like everybody else."

God wasn't quite finished singling us out. Imagine our surprise once we discovered we were expecting not one, but two babies—one born of my heart, one born of my flesh. This time, we received more than a few raised eyebrows. Family, friends, and adoption caseworkers were concerned and skeptical at best, while others thought we were crazy. I was overwhelmed but excited, secure in the knowledge of God's plan. God had chosen me to be part of something so amazing!

When I arrived in China to embrace my new daughter, I left my newborn baby behind. I missed one baby terribly while trying desperately to bond with the next. Never had I felt so frightened or so alone. Once I returned home, I felt isolated, knowing that even the most empathetic of my friends and family could not relate. At that point I wanted nothing more than to be normal. The cost of a remarkable life was much too high.

As the months went by, our family settled into a routine, but life never returned to normal. My family had been changed forever, and more importantly, so had I. As one who could appreciate the cost of obedience, I was better equipped to follow Christ. As one whose faith had triumphed over fear, I had become a better witness. I had learned to walk in the footsteps of my unconventional Savior. The more I refused to look like everybody else, the more I took on the image of Christ.

Pamela Watts is an author, speaker, and mother of four beautiful children. She enjoys sharing adventures in parenting, specializing in depictions of everyday life viewed through the lens of God's extraordinary Truth. Pamela lives with her family in Waco, Texas. Learn more about her unconventional life at www.pamrichardswatts.wordpress.com.

The Reboot Button

Yvonne Ortega

HAVE YOU EVER known a time when you needed to change your way of thinking? Did you ever wish you could wave a magic wand and reboot your mind as easily as you reboot your computer? I have.

Within weeks of one another, I lost two aunts, my mother, and my only child. For almost two years I felt overwhelmed with grief. Everywhere I went reminded me of my family. I heard music or watched a movie and thought of them. I could hardly walk past my son's bedroom without crying. Mother's Day, their birthdays, and anniversaries of their deaths left me in a fetal position sobbing.

Mom was my best friend, my cheerleader, my encourager. Who would care now the way Mom did?

My son's death meant more than the loss of my only child. It also meant I would never be a grandmother. I would never carry a brag book of pictures of my grandchildren. I would never buy clothes or toys for them.

That's when I knew I had to reboot my mind. I needed to change my thinking.

I started the process by attending Compassionate Friends, a support group for parents who've lost a child. The people were wonderful. They listened. They understood. However, they met only once a month. I needed more support than that.

Other than journaling and writing a weekly devotion I was committed to, I couldn't write. My mind felt paralyzed. Even a blog post challenged me.

An acquaintance told me about Grief Share, a Christian support group that met weekly. Their key phrase was "a new normal." I didn't want "a new normal." I wanted my family back. Of course, that wasn't going to happen, but over time, the idea of "a new normal" became more acceptable. Maybe I could do this after all.

A friend on a prayer loop said she would pray with me for thirty days. She suggested I pray Psalm 91 every day. She challenged me to break the devil's hold on me by praying in the name and authority of Jesus Christ and asking God to replace Satan's turmoil with God's peace.

Gradually I realized I had been stuck in the pattern of this world in regard to grief. We all come with an expiration date. As a Christian, my ultimate citizenship is in heaven. So is that of my loved ones who know the Lord. I'd overlooked the fact Jesus promised he was going back to heaven to prepare a place for us to be with him. I did have hope.

Every time I prayed Psalm 91 and other Scriptures, I renewed my mind. My hunger for the Bible returned as did the desire to write and speak publicly.

I completed a manuscript I hadn't worked on in two years. I couldn't type fast enough. Joy and satisfaction overflowed the day I submitted the completed manuscript to three publishers for consideration.

I accepted speaking engagements in my state and others. I looked forward to each opportunity, and the joy of speaking for the Lord returned.

Through God's grace, I discovered the secret to changing my thinking. I found the reboot button. As I renewed my mind, I found out how good, pleasing, and perfect God's will is for my life. This doesn't mean I won't have any more troubles. I will face many more challenges. However, my prayer is that next time, I will be quicker to turn my back on Satan's lies and cling to God's Word. That is the only way I can renew my mind.

Yvonne Ortega is a national bilingual speaker, author of *Finding Hope for Your Journey through Breast Cancer*, counselor, teacher, and host of "Hope for the Journey with Yvonne Ortega," a blogtalkradio show on breast cancer, addiction, and other types of trauma. Her website is www.yvonneortega.com. Her new blog is yvonneortega.blogspot.com

Ruth Márquez West

The Prayer Circle

I ESCAPED TO my truck to shout at God in private. In neighborhood traffic, I lost myself in grief, waiting for red lights to turn green. Here, desperation was at least confined to the cab of a Tacoma pickup where my children could not hear me doubt my Savior out loud.

Though I was known as a "prayer warrior," as was my mother before me, my life was caught up in a tailspin of failure. Facing the spiritual defeat of a crumbling marriage, I could not hear God above my mournful distraction. In the midst of the chaos, messengers of prayer found their way into my life at pivotal moments.

"The Lord woke me up last night and I began writing and praying for you," a teacher at my children's new school said to me. The pages of handwritten Scripture she handed me were proof of her prayerful labor. I was astonished at the care and detail of her writing, evidence of long and reflective intercession on my behalf. Humbled by the prayers of a woman who did not know me well, I experienced God's personal touch just when I thought He was blind to my suffering.

This willing prayer warrior for God, and others like her, went out of their way to let me know, "The Lord put you on my heart and I am praying for you." The thought that my heavenly Father was nudging others to pray for me was life-changing. Slowly, even in my pain, my mind was renewed and I began to see the deep needs of others.

"They don't expect her to make it through the afternoon," a member of my new church indicated in her brief phone call. I fell to my knees, knowing firsthand that God could use my prayers for a woman I did not know well. It was the first of many prayer requests to come as the Lord continued to include me in His transforming work. Whether emails from women on the verge of divorce, conversations with parents at the end of their rope, or news of illness or death, prayer became much more than volunteer ministry. It began to set the rhythm of my life.

The Prayer Circle

Despite the upheaval in my own soon-to-be-single-again life, the Lord placed more and more people on my heart for prayer. I saw that responding to His prompting blessed me in a surprising way. The more I turned from angst over my circumstances to focus on the lives of others, my heart blossomed.

My emergence from a heap of sadness and loss can only be explained by the mysteries of God renewing my mind through prayer—from others, for others, and with others.

"We forgot that Zak is sick," my daughter noted, disappointed that we did not pray together for our favorite little neighbor. Exhausted after the long day, we ended our family prayer time with his upcoming surgery on our hearts. My children's commitment to intercede for our little friend removed any doubt that our family had come full circle—we had been transformed by prayer.

Ruth Márquez West prayed with her parents as a little girl. An active intercessor, Ruth points others toward corporate and individual prayer. Ms. Márquez West writes articles, devotions, and books-in-progress to minister to single-again believers and their families in addition to writing and editing in communications and public relations.

Lawrence J. Clark

The Church of Oscar

TWO BIG SMOKIES, extra onions on one, no mustard on the other. One Mrs. Smokie extra pickles!"

The cashier shouted her order in a thick southern accent that I could barely understand. Two weeks earlier I had moved to Knoxville, Tennessee, on a whim.

I was nineteen and single, and with my choleric/sanguine personality it sounded like a fun thing to do. I was a hard worker, so I found a job as a short-order cook at the Smokey Mountain Market, where I met my new boss, Oscar.

"You need to get yourself a coat," he announced as I stood shivering in the damp, pre-dawn air. "Let's get you some coffee."

"Sounds good, eh," I said.

"New England?"

"Ayuh—Maine."

"Thought so. Welcome to the real America, Yankee Boy."

His broad smile disarmed me, and Oscar soon taught me everything he knew; I learned to cook food I had never even eaten, like grits.

"Blech!!" I said, spitting them back out. "How can you eat this mush?"

"It's an acquired taste, Yank," Oscar laughed, slapping his thigh through his gravy-splotched apron.

One morning, while rolling out biscuit dough, my curiosity got the best of me.

"Oscar, how come you're working here? When I'm your age, I plan to be a millionaire living on my own island."

"Good question. I wasn't always a cook; I was once a bank president."

"C'mon . . ."

114

"I'm serious. Worked my way through college, got promoted, and married the day after graduation."

"Cool."

"Came from a mining family. I was the first to graduate college."

"Good for you—bank president, wow . . ."

"Working that hard is stressful, though. Started drinking every night. I made life miserable for my wife and kids. Soon I was out of control, but somehow kept getting promoted."

"Cool."

"Maybe. I had the money, the company car, the country club . . ."

"I want all that!"

"Everything has a price, Yank. My wife and kids despised me. The Bible tells us that the root of all evil is the love of money."

"You believe all that Bible stuff?"

"Yes, sir. Didn't always, though. I went to Sunday school, but after college Christianity lost its relevance, just a way for politicians and corporations to keep ignorant folks dreaming about a better life in la-la land while they laughed all the way to the bank, my bank. I laughed, too, and treated the 'little people' like peasants."

"I can't imagine that."

"Thanks, but I didn't change on my own. One night, after several cocktails, I had a severe heart attack and slammed into a tree. The doc said I'd die within a year if I didn't quit my job. I realized power or money wouldn't do me any good six feet under."

"So what happened?"

"Drove straight to my boyhood church, sat for a long time, and thought about what a mess I was. I tried to ask Jesus for forgiveness, but all I could do was cry. Afterward, though, a giant weight was suddenly lifted."

"I get that," I said, then told him about the time a year earlier when I was selling vacuums door to door. One night, after I finished my sales pitch, a guy got his Bible and explained how everyone's a sinner, but God sent his Son to die so we could be free."

"But I don't see you going to church now, Yank," he observed. "And spending your time in clubs down on the strip isn't exactly the life Jesus wants for you."

"But that's where all my friends are, Oscar. You old guys can hang out in church, but that's not much fun for us."

"There are other ways to spend time with Him. I pray every morning at work – one of the things I love about this job. People leave me alone, for the most part."

"Except me, of course."

"Ah, you're alright, for a Yankee, anyway," he grinned. "Now enough of this chit-chat – we've only got fifteen minutes to finish these biscuits."

Transformed

We shared many conversations after that, and Oscar taught me lessons I remember to this day. I started attending a young adult Bible study, and a year later earned a scholarship to a Christian college where I continued my transformation into the likeness of Christ, a process that continues thirty years later.

And I will never forget my very first church, the Church of Oscar.

Lawrence J. Clark is an author, speaker, and songwriter who frequently speaks and performs in schools, churches, and libraries. He is co-founder, with his wife Kristen, of HisWitness.org and NewBeginningsMarriage.org, for which he writes a regular column based on personality theory, marriage, and men's issues.

Judy Wade

Stronger in the Broken Places

"We are hard pressed on every side, but not crushed; perplexed, but not in despair, persecuted, but not abandoned; struck down, but not destroyed."

—2 Corinthians 4:8-9

MOMENTS BEFORE IMPACT, I woke to my friend's scream and the sounds of crashing metal and shattering glass. The van ran into a ditch, hit a culvert pipe, and catapulted us into a series of end-over-end rolls. Our bodies tumbled around the van like ragdolls in a dryer with each flip. An eerie silence followed as the van came to rest upside down on the rain-drenched ground.

After such a violent crash, the stillness seemed somewhat out of place, but I knew it was God's peace surrounding me. Soon the quietness was pierced by the sounds of sirens as emergency lights flashed through the broken windows.

We were heading home from a women's retreat we had conducted the night before. I spent the weekend teaching the Word of God and encouraging broken women. Trusting God in every situation was the last message I gave. Was it possible that this accident was a test to determine whether I had embraced my own teaching? *God, are you sure you have the right person for this test?* Now the word "broken" was about to take on an entirely new meaning.

Upon arriving at the hospital, I was immediately taken to x-ray, still firmly bound to the gurney. The pain in my back intensified and felt as if a thousand needles penetrated my skin. The doctor walked into the room and said, "Mrs. Wade, you have several crushed vertebrae in your back and three broken bones in your neck. We are not equipped for your type of injuries. We are transferring you to a trauma center where the neurosurgeon will evaluate you. We will not be able to give you pain medication before you are transported. I am sorry but there is nothing more we can do." *Did he actually say broken neck and back?*

Transformed

God, I know you are with me, I prayed. *You have not forsaken me, Thank You for sparing our lives and allowing my friend to walk away with minor injuries. Lord, help me to praise You through this situation. Grant me Your peace.*

I opened my eyes to find my husband leaning over me. With tears in his eyes, he spoke with a gentle, yet confident voice, "Judy, God has already told me you are going to be okay. He has assured me you are in His hands." I felt God's love flow through my husband as he put my motionless hand in his.

In the following weeks and months, God's faithfulness and grace amazed us. My six- month checkup with the neurosurgeon proved God is still in the healing business. The doctor said, "I am looking at fully developed bone, and this is not even medically possible. Someone has worked on you besides me." The Great Physician had placed His healing touch on my body.

Not only had God healed me physically, but my spiritual transformation led me on a journey of faith. I now trust God at a deeper level than I could have ever imagined.

What appears to the natural eye to wreak havoc in our lives may only be a detour to bring us to a place of fulfilling God's purpose. I learned to praise God in the good times and in my challenges. My accident was definitely not part of my plan, but I can honestly say it has made me stronger in the broken places.

Judy Wade of Cumming, Georgia, conducts weekend retreats and is a contributing writer for *Arise Magazine.* She and her husband are co-founders of Heart 2 Heart Ministries. Their retreats are conducted in their ministry home appropriately named, "A Taste of Heaven," located in the north Georgia mountains. www.heart2heartministries.org.

Kathy Carlton Willis

Fairy Spa Frog

MY WHITE KNIGHT gifted me with a half-day at the spa for our twenty-sixth wedding anniversary. Yesterday was my day to ride in the white horseless carriage (a.k.a. 2002 minivan) to the midday delight.

First, Spa-girl #1 escorted me into the miracle-vault for my facial. Soothing music lulled my stress away, as various potions and lotions were applied to my face, neck, and shoulders. Oh the wonder-working power in her touch! It was simply amazing. I promised myself I would stay in the moment for the entire spa experience, not allowing my mind to fuss over the "what ifs" of my future, nor retreating backward in my mind to any regrets.

Spa-girl #1 tagged off to Spa-girl #2 and we determined to wash away the gray. What gray? She wasn't a miracle worker; she was a magician. She made things disappear. If only she could do the same for a few extra pounds!

Next came a Lisa Rinna hairstyle. Do styling lessons come with the package? I'm quite certain I will need a tutorial on how to use a flat iron.

Then Spa-girl #2 performed the modern-day equivalent of foot-washing. The spa pedicure. Mmmm…'nuff said!

Last night I went to bed feeling like a princess, but today when I woke up the fairytale charm was gone.

All that pulling and tugging of various tissues released toxins I didn't even know I had. My eyes from the eyebrows to the eyelashes resembled red globes and my face ballooned to Wicked Stepmother status.

I guess I forgot to look at the clock. Apparently at midnight the princess dust wore off and I turned back into a frog!

This princess business had an expiration date. Reality of my life. Except for one arena—my life with Christ.

I am now and for always a daughter of the King with all the privileges included. The "toxins" released by His touch aren't released in me but out of me. I'm freed from their influence. And I need not worry that I'll awake in the morning with the wonder of His love worn off. He is mine and I am His—forever.

Father God, I thank You for loving me with an unfailing love, steadfast, enduring—with mercies that are new every morning and hope that lasts an eternity.

"O give thanks unto the Lord; for he is good: for his mercy endureth for ever. O give thanks unto the God of gods; for his mercy endureth for ever…to him who alone doeth great wonders; for his mercy endureth for ever."

—Psalm 136:1-2, 4 KJV

Kathy Carlton Willis gets jazzed fiddling with words as publicist, author, speaker, and more. She shines, whether she's shining the light on God's writers and speakers, or reflecting God's light during her speaking engagements. She's all about "aha" light bulb moments, and sometimes spa fairy transformations. http://www.kathycarltonwillis.com/.

Susan Titus Osborn

Perfect Shells and Broken Pieces

IWALKED ALONG the beach one autumn morning, hoping to find shells for my collection. The summer tourists had gone home, and the kids had returned to school. The beach was deserted except for an elderly couple walking hand-in-hand and a man scavenging with a metal detector. I seemed to be the only person searching for shells.

However, all I could find were broken pieces. I kicked at the sand in frustration. The broken shells reminded me of the fragmented pieces of my own life since the breakup of my marriage.

The wind whipped my hair and sent a chill down my back. I pulled my sweatshirt around me and kept walking. Somehow, I hoped my brisk pace would help me leave my problems behind to be swept out with the tide. Instead, the waves kept bringing in more and more broken shells.

Then I paused and cried out, "Where are you, Lord? I don't know what to do. I feel so broken."

I resumed walking, trying to gain some perspective on my situation. What had happened to my perfect little family of four? Like the shells, my hopes and dreams for the future had been dashed on the rocks.

God seemed silent. Yet, I sensed the fault was mine, not His. I wasn't seeking His guidance so much as I was venting my anger by shouting.

Another wave surged on the shore, and I continued my search. To my surprise, this one brought in a beautiful whole shell. Scooping it up in my hand, I turned it over and noticed how perfectly God had formed it. In the midst of all this brokenness was wholeness.

Perhaps God would transform me and make me whole, too. However, I needed to do my part. Instead of dwelling on my problems and unmet expectations, I needed to plan for the future. I no longer had a husband, but I did have two wonderful teenage boys. The three of us were still a family.

We could build on what we had. We could love and encourage each other. We could laugh and plan inexpensive outings together. We could look to the future, knowing God would guide our path if only we allowed Him.

Perhaps, if I stopped shouting at God, I would be able to hear Him speak. Once again, I looked down at the perfect shell in my hand and smiled. Had God already spoken?

As I look back over that occasion that happened twenty-five years ago, I can see how God transformed my life. He took the broken pieces of my shattered life and once again made me whole. Today I am happily remarried to a godly man, Dick Osborn, and I once again feel the peace and presence of God's love in my life.

Susan Titus Osborn is director of the Christian Communicator Manuscript Critique Service. She has authored 30 books. Susan is a member of The CLASSeminar staff and is a CLASS speaker. As an author, Susan represents New Hope Publishers. She lives in Fullerton, California, with her husband Dick. Susan can be reached at www.Christiancommunicator.com.

Rebecca Dowden

On Bloody Knees

DARLA BETH FLEW around the corner on her bright red Schwinn bicycle. I felt love and envy at the same time. "How do you like my new bike, Becky?" Her enormous grin told me she wasn't waiting for my answer. "My dad got this bike for me, and I didn't even have to use training wheels. He says I'm a natural!" She circled me one more time and then pedaled out of sight.

I raced into my house. "Mom, Mom, Mom!" Frantically running from room to room, I searched for my mother.

Hearing the desperation in my voice, she rushed out of the laundry room. "What in the world is wrong, sweetie?"

"Mom, I really need a bike!"

"A bike?"

"Yes! Today! Now! Can we go when Daddy gets home?"

"What's this all about, Becky? Why the sudden need for a bike?"

I thought it over for a minute and then I blurted out the truth. "Darla Beth has one, and I want one too. I'm old enough to ride a bike. Mom! Please!"

Unfortunately, I didn't get the object of my desire that night; however, the next week I received an early birthday present: a pink Schwinn with a banana seat, sissy bar, and pink handle bar streamers.

I woke up early the next morning and rushed out to the garage. My anticipation to climb onto my chariot and let the streamers of glory blow in the wind was almost more than I could bear. Unfortunately, when the garage door swung open, I stopped in horror.

"Daddy, what have you done?" My father, wrench in hand, stood beaming at me. He gave me his best Vanna White gesture towards my new bike and waited for my response.

"Why, why, did you put training wheels on my new beautiful bike?" I sobbed kneeling down beside my tainted new friend. My dad put his steady hand on my trembling shoulder.

"Honey, these will help you learn how to ride. They will keep you balanced."

"I can ride without those, Daddy! I'm a big girl!"

Without a word, my dad removed the training wheels. Then, as he handed me the bike, he asked me, "How about I give you a hand until you get used to riding?"

"No, I can do this, Dad. I know how! I'll be a natural just like Darla Beth!" I mounted my new steed with confidence, but before I could reach the end of the driveway, my uncontrollable wobbling threw me off the bike and onto the unforgiving concrete. As I lay there in a heap of defeat with bloody knees and a bruised ego, I realized how much I really did need my dad.

Within a flash, Dad scooped me up in his arms and tended to my scrapes and bruises.

My relationship with my heavenly father hasn't been much different. In various seasons of my life, I've also told God, "I can do this. I'm a natural!" I wanted to do things on my own, solve my own problems, and be enough for whatever situation in my life. Self-reliance invaded every thought.

My self-reliance didn't transform into dependence on God until I found myself on bloody knees again in my early twenties. During those years, I struggled with deep depression and tried to muster up enough emotional strength to be happy. I asked God to give me peace and take away the depression, but the second those words left my mouth, I resumed my mission to fix myself. However, my mission failed again and again.

Like a little girl with bloody knees and a broken heart who learns to trust her father's guidance, I realize my heavenly Father is the only one who can hold me up. God delivered me from the depths of depression. Even though I don't live next door to Darla Beth anymore, I still face many people and trials that tempt me to go it alone. However, these days, I stop and remember my wobbly insufficiencies and fall to my knees asking God for his steady, loving hand.

Dr. Rebecca Dowden loves helping people learn how to open their hearts and develop deeper relationships with God. She is a Christian radio show host, writer, counselor, and professor. When she is not in front of the computer, she loves spending time with her husband and her chocolate lab.

Ruth Ann Dalley

The Holy Spirit Renewed My Life

CHRISTMAS EVE, I sat alone in church. During the traditional service, I felt the presence of the Holy Spirit. I prayed my storms would stop. Peace flowed though me. His healing transformed me, and my fear diminished.

I heard about the Holy Spirit all my life. However, through high school and college no one taught me what the Holy Spirit does in my life.

After retirement came my "perfect storm." Unlike the movie, I faced five crises instead of three in four years. The first storm gathered as I cared for my husband, and my elderly mother who was in a facility. I became depressed when I faced their deaths, only three months apart.

The second storm came one month later when the massive Witch Creek Fire raged. I stayed five days at a motel. The repair, restoration, and resale of my California house lasted four years.

The third storm came when I started to lose blood but didn't know it. For six months, I lost blood one drop at a time. The doctors diagnosed me with G.A.V.E. disease, a rare stomach disorder. I endured five to six endoscopy laser treatments to stop the blood flow.

When my sister-in-law asked me to help her lobby for the retention of the senior bus service, I faced my fourth storm. Although the city cut the transit bus service, the Jewish Center started a small transit system in the area for senior citizens.

Exhausted and confused from the previous storms, I faced yet another. One of my ministers told me I needed counseling. My fifth storm.

During treatment, I learned from the Bible that the Holy Spirit is a gift from God to Christians. The Holy Spirit transformed my life from the inside out.

The chaos stopped. I clung to my faith, but my hope waivered.

Transformed

I knew the worst was over, but where was God's will in my life? Even though I studied the Bible and prayed, no answer came. I continued to search for His will. The Holy Spirit guided, counseled, and showed me God's will for me to become a grateful servant to the Lord.

I attended Florence Littauer's Personalities Plus Seminar, Marcia Ramsland's Simplify Your Life Seminar, and three Christian writers' conferences to learn how to walk in God's will and understand myself and others.

God's transformation through the Holy Spirit is life changing. I now surrender to God's will, not mine, daily. The Holy Spirit renewed my mind and continues to do so.

Ruth Ann Dalley lives in the San Diego area. A retired teacher, she taught different subjects at various grade levels. She enjoys her two Tibetan Spaniels and knits items for premature babies for children's hospitals all over the country. Photography is another of her hobbies.

Kathy Lynn Hall

The Night I Put the Gun Down

I PRAYED, "LORD, You see who has a gun in his hand right now ready to kill someone. Please, Lord, cause him to put the gun down. Thank You, in Jesus' name."

Weeks later, I asked Joey, "Tell me what brings you here for help?"

"My family was told to move from Los Angeles County and never come back. We were members of the MS13 gang and always in trouble. I grew up without a dad. He was mostly in prison. My uncle is in prison in Guatemala for murdering seven people. Gangs are all I have ever known.

"One night it was my turn to kill a cop.

"We got pulled over. I had the gun in my hand. But, something happened that I couldn't explain. I hid the gun. I was arrested and sitting before my probation officer in Reno, Nevada, when she told me there were people in New Mexico that might be able to help me. I went back to my cell and did what I always did—counted the bricks in the wall. I knew I needed to change. My probation officer was a Christian and said these people were Christians. Then I talked to you and Brother Lin, (my husband), and decided to come."

That was the first time I had heard him tell what happened. Faith and joy began to rise in me as I remembered the night I had prayed for a person to put the gun down. God heard my prayers. I didn't have to know the name of the person I was praying for, or where he was. God did this. He wanted me to know how involved He is in the details of my daily life! There were things I prayed about that just didn't seem to be getting God's attention. At that moment, I knew I had His attention and He was at work answering all my prayers. His love is unfailing! He hears my loudest cries and my softest whispers.

Joey memorized Jeremiah 29:11, "'For, I know the plans I have for you,' says the Lord. 'they are plans for good and not for disaster, to give you a future and a hope.'" He learned that God gave His only Son to die on the cross for him and if he believed, God wanted to give him eternal life. Joey drew a cross. On it he wrote everything he could think of that he had done wrong (even when he knew better). He prayed and asked Jesus to forgive him. Then he thanked Jesus for suffering and dying on the cross for his sins. Joey wept as he felt the heavy burden of sin lifted from him.

There was no more guilt, no more fear, no more hate! He felt love filling his soul like never before. He stood up, arms raised, praising God for placing him on the path of righteousness.

"Now, I know God has a destiny for me! I want to tell others what He has done for me." Every morning and every night he read his Bible. He read, "And so, dear brothers and sisters, I plead with you to give your bodies to God because of all He has done for you. Let them be a living and holy sacrifice—the kind He will find acceptable. This is truly the way to worship Him. Don't copy the behavior and customs of this world, but let God transform you into a new person by changing the way you think. Then you will learn to know God's will for you, which is good and pleasing and perfect" (Romans 12:1-2 NLT).

Joey's passion for Christ grew every day. He soon looked different. His face reflected the joy of his salvation. He talked differently. Everything he said made you feel better. Scowls were replaced with smiles.

Several years have passed since Joey's life was transformed through the power of Jesus Christ. Today, Joey, his wife, and two little girls are involved in church planting in Las Vegas, Nevada, reaching out to teens. May our Lord Jesus receive all the glory and honor His precious name deserves!

The names in this story have been changed.

Co-founder and Director of Teen Challenge (New Mexico), Kathy Lynn Hall also speaks for Bible Studies and women's events. She writes prayers and devotions to intercede for Christians who have no words. Her life message is an example of God's power in everyday life. For more ministry information, contact lmhklh@msn.com

Nancy Davis Biffle

Nothing Changed But Me

IWHINED TO myself. Life was hard the first year my husband went back to school. We moved hundreds of miles from family and friends. We were always short on time, money, or both. I was the special education teacher on a campus for K-8thgrades—a demanding and exhausting job. Twenty-one special students filled my classroom, nine to eleven years old, and tagged with labels no longer politically correct. I taught all levels and all subjects with very few materials and no teacher's aide.

These children shouldn't have been in the same classroom and I felt overwhelmed.

I remember sitting in the first faculty meeting when our principal announced the school-wide goal for standardized testing. "Excuse me," I responded. "I thought I heard you say our goal was fifty percent of our students would make fifty percent on the test."

"Yes, that's correct." I tried not to show my shock at such low expectations.

I found the school atmosphere stressful and depressing. The neighborhood had earned a reputation for gang activity and intimidation. When my students talked to me, their lives sounded like the national news. One little guy named Pedro confided how the two families living in his house associated with different gangs. A cousin protected Pedro from his own brother. Another child, Glenn knew where guns were hidden and Jose's brother was wounded in a drive-by shooting.

My heart broke when one of my fourth-grade girls retracted her story of incest because mom didn't want to lose the stepfather's income. Thieves vandalized our school and stole computers and other equipment including several personal possessions. These events were my student's everyday reality and were becoming mine. When arsonists set fire to a neighboring school, my principal insisted I quit staying late—a first.

With rival gangs in school, even a simple choice could be life-threatening. Once, police locked down our campus because one gang threatened to shoot anyone wearing the opposing gang's color. Students and teachers nervously waited in classrooms while police and administrators kept in touch by radios. What can you say to a sobbing child who happened to wear the wrong color? The hours passed at glacial speed until finally police released us to go home. Fortunately, no one was hurt—at least physically.

Additionally, we missed family, had few friends, little money, and continually experienced the strain that accompanied George's doctoral program. My patience often ran thin for our three children ages three, eleven, and fifteen. My stressed body broke out in painful boils, mostly hidden by clothing. I dreaded my workday alarm and begged God for relief.

So life continued, until our first desert Christmas when George gave me the New Testament on tape.

Listening to Scripture during my long commute provided some encouragement. Then one day God used Philippians 4:8-9 to drag me from my well of self-pity. "Finally, brethren, whatever is true, whatever is honorable, whatever is right, whatever is pure, whatever is lovely, whatever is of good repute, if there is any excellence and if anything worthy of praise, dwell on these things. The things you have learned and received and heard and seen in me, practice these things, and the God of peace will be with you" (NASB).

I eagerly turned to Philippians 4:8-9 in my Bible. The word "anything" leaped from the page into my heart. "Is there *anything* lovely or good about this job?" My first dubious answer was "There must be." I longed to focus on any shred of good in my situation, rather than dwell on what appeared impossible.

I replaced negative thoughts with Scripture and positive truth about the situation. Nevertheless, some days challenged me to find even a tiny thing worthy of praise.

I prayed to see these children through Christ's eyes and exchange His thoughts for mine. Although our own kids qualified for the government reduced lunch program, my students considered me rich. Our house was crowded, but there were no bars on our doors and windows. In spite of multiple disabilities, my students had a sense of humor and compassion for others.

My pity turned to love for those special students. I became more creative and consistent in classroom management. The boils disappeared and my patience increased. Amazingly, nothing in my situation changed except my perspective and belief. God answered prayers I hadn't even known to pray.

I finally understood—my job didn't need transforming—I did.

Nancy Davis Biffle is a freelance writer living in Texas.

Connie Leonard

Faith Journey

"'For I know the plans I have for you,' declares the Lord, 'plans to prosper you and not to harm you, plans to give you hope and a future.'"

—Jeremiah 29:11

MY FAITH JOURNEY began before I was born when my mother was six months pregnant, and she was seriously injured in an automobile accident. The doctors didn't give much hope for my survival, but God had other plans. The elders from her church came to the hospital, laid hands on her, and prayed for us. Three months later, the nuns and priests at St. Mary's all proclaimed me perfectly healthy and normal, the miracle baby, and a special gift from God. At thirteen months old, I contracted double bronchial pneumonia, with temperatures spiking to 106 degrees. Once again, the doctors didn't give hope for my survival, but God had other plans.

My mother passed her faith to our family. She took us to church and when I was six, my father accepted Christ as his personal Savior. Our family enjoyed a smooth journey being involved in church and becoming friends with the pastor and his family. Then came a major roadblock. Conflicts in the church caused an ugly battle and my parents became disillusioned and dropped out of church.

Our family journeyed in the desert for several years. Renewal came through a little country church, and we once again walked with Christ. I loved singing hymns, Sunday school, and vacation Bible school. When I was eleven, Christ spoke to my heart and invited me to accept Him as my Savior. According to the doctrine of the church, we had to repent, accept Christ as Savior, be baptized, and *maybe* if our good works outweighed our bad, we could get into heaven. At eleven, I wasn't ready for such responsibility, but God was ready for me. Although I was afraid to walk down the aisle, I took that first step and God carried me the rest of the way. Filled with happiness, I began my personal journey with Christ.

Transformed

When I entered junior high school, I learned about Youth for Christ. Youth rallies, retreats, Bible study, and prayer filled me with excitement. Unfortunately our sponsor moved away. Our group disbanded, sending me back on a dirt road, going to church only on Easter and a few other times a year.

A young pastor started a new church near our home. Because of his outreach and excitement for God, I found myself zooming along a super highway. If nobody else in my family wanted to go to church, I drove myself and found joy in the journey.

When I was sixteen, I met the love of my life, a good-looking preacher's son. We fell in love, married, and I joined his church. We faithfully attended every service, and my dream of the family walking into church together hand-in-hand became a reality. We read and studied the Bible, prayed, and passed that legacy on to our children. Life was good, a smooth, scenic drive.

But God had higher plans. He called my husband into the ministry. He quit his job to attend college and seminary, and I went to work. So began an uncertain journey up a windy road where we couldn't see beyond the next bend. With each turn, Christ's light shone through the darkness and carried us safely to the next point. He proved Himself faithful by providing for our needs in His way, His time.

Reflecting over thirty-six years of ministry and four pastorates, our journey has been a rollercoaster ride. Occasionally a few stretches of gentle country road carried us contentedly along. We've reached mountain tops only to plummet to the depths with deaths, disappointments, betrayals, and cancer.

Faith is a transforming journey with God. If it weren't for the storms, we couldn't see Christ walk on water. If we didn't fall on our faces in the mud, He couldn't lift us up and put us back on solid ground. If our hearts didn't break, He couldn't wrap His comforting arms around us. If we weren't burdened, He couldn't give us rest. May we relax and experience His joy in the journey.

Connie Lewis Leonard lives in Texas with her husband of over forty years. They have two grown children, two grandchildren, and three dogs. Her hobbies include reading, baking, gardening, and scrapbooking. Since retiring from teaching, she is pursuing a life-long dream and passion for writing.

Robin Stanley

It's All a Part of the Process

THE SILENCE OF desert sanctuary hangs in quiet overtones above the roar of the 747. I settle into my seat over the wing, expecting my flight home to include a long nap. Instead, my heart awakens to consider the wind. Not the wind rushing past my window, but the strength of a gentle Wind that scatters seeds across a dusty landscape.

Seeds of life. Words of life.

Several words hover from the week, waiting to light long upon my tongue. I gather them in, chew on them a while. One phrase lingers longer than expected, leaving a question swirling around its delivery. When I attempted to express the soul-impact of the previous days at the Ghost Ranch, a friend replied, "It's all a part of the process." At the time, I smiled and nodded in agreement. But one question looms: "the process of what?"

As I catch the Wind and bend low to hear its response, I see the surface of the word "process." I like the way it hits my lips, eases through my teeth. It implies movement. It seems positive. My breath hesitates on the final "ssss," releasing the steam of momentum. It feels hard.

My mind wanders back to another dusty landscape where I might uncover definition. Perhaps I will manage to get around "hard." Memory lands in Jos, Nigeria. A country full of "hard."

From the point of decision to go, that trip managed to press my knees into the ground. *Jesus, Nigeria? Really? But, I....*

No amount of stammered resistance changed His mind. The invitation came. I accepted. With eighteen others from three other states, we ministered in three Nigerian cities, calling women to see each other and walk together in truth and love. My skin began to stretch. Growing pains purposed their way to the surface. "It's all a part of the process." I need to go deeper.

The path wound upward around boulders and under broad-leafed trees. Earth's dust clung to our damp clothes in the late morning heat. Homemade striped canopies peered over the crest of the hill. Rhythms of African talking drums, bongos, and beaded shakers pulsed through the crusted air. My spirit filled. Anticipation swelled.

We rounded the bend. My heart burst. Dozens of women erupted in praise, dancing, and clapping, ushering us into an irretrievable moment. An explosion of beauty and grace, the sounds, the images of these women whose life stories spoke to the horrors of AIDS, seared love upon my heart. Tears came. And kept coming. Love pierces darkness and binds all fear. "It's all a part of the process." Probing. Listening. Longing. There's more. I lean in.

Resolute and graceful, a woman clothed in red stepped to the front of the awning where our group sat. Her face worn, but softened by love, lifted heavenward. Her words spilled with assurance that can only come from surviving a storm through which you discover you're made to bend, not to break.

Gloria's story flows from unimaginable circumstances. She is HIV positive. The disease she shared with her husband already claimed his life and threatened to consume hers. Gloria testifies with every fiber of her well-lived life. She tells of a heroic rescue—not of flesh, but of blood. She had given herself to death. But Jesus found her on the streets of Jos. He snatched her from the pit of hell and set her feet to dancing.

She overflows with hope, restored by the blood of Christ and awash in beauty she cannot contain. Gloria, and others like her, spill love from their grateful hearts to others in need—even one such as me. The cycle of grace comes around full once it's both received and given. Freedom experienced releases the dance. Unrestrained. Unencumbered. Without pretense or notion of fame. "It's all a part of the process." I hear the ease of the Wind as it scatters these now life-giving words across the dusty landscape of my heart.

"It's all a part of the process…of being beautiful." *He makes everything beautiful in its time* (Ecclesiastes 3:11, NASB). Everything.

Robin Stanley comes alongside writers and speakers through relationship-based coaching and representation to guide them through the processes of discerning, releasing, and distributing their God-given gifts. A former acquisitions editor and founder of o3-free, Robin is a freelance writer, speaker, and worship leader. She serves on the faculty and board of directors for CLASSEMINARS, Inc.

Gary L. Leonard

Fortified, Not Forgotten

SERVING GOD IS not without pain. The summer of 1983 was a time of transition; I felt I had been left in the desert and forgotten. Recently graduated from Southwestern Baptist Theological Seminary in Fort Worth, Texas, no doors of opportunity opened for me. As our friends were called to ministry positions and moved away, we wondered if God had forgotten us. Worse yet, if He even cared.

As I struggled with my own disappointments, despair, and feelings of abandonment, I began to doubt the faithfulness of God. He showed me a passage of scripture which became a source of inspiration and encouragement. In Jeremiah 15, as the prophet contemplated his call and his ministry, he complained that God had lied to him and caused him great pain. In His response to Jeremiah, God simply spoke these words: "If you return, then I will restore you—Before Me you will stand; And if you extract the precious from the worthless, You will become My spokesman" (Jeremiah 15:19). Following His rebuke, God gives him a wonderful promise: "Then I will make you to this people a fortified wall of bronze; And though they fight against you, They will not prevail over you; For I am with you to save you And to deliver you, so I will deliver you from the hand of the wicked, And I will redeem you from the grasp of the violent" (Jeremiah 15:20-21).

God's message to this man was the same He wanted me to hear. "When you repent of your unfaithfulness, I will be able to use you in My master plan." We can't be successful if our lives are filled with unfaithful behavior such as doubt, impatience, selfishness, or any other form of rebellion against God.

Even though it was a painful lesson, I realized that before any Christian can be strong in the power of the Lord, he must learn to trust God completely. The pain in serving God is not His punishment, but is His way of making us tough enough to be useful when the going gets rough. In the transforming process, God makes us into a fortified wall of bronze so we can stand up against the evil and the sin we will face. God hasn't called us to be powder puffs, but to be warriors against the powers and the principalities of this world.

The Apostle Paul made it clear in Ephesians 6:12-13a: "For our struggle is not against flesh and blood, but against the rulers, against the powers, against the world forces of this darkness, against the spiritual forces of wickedness in the heavenly places. Therefore, take up the full armor of God…" (NASB)

God's message from this passage spoke to me; the darkness of my mood was illuminated by His marvelous light. Before the summer of 1983 was over, God placed us in the right place at the right time. As we serve our Lord, the hurts have not decreased and the disappointments have not quit coming, but one thing I know for sure, His strength is made perfect in my weakness. God did not abandon me, and the lessons of the faith that lead to transformation have never stopped. He delivers me from the hand of the wicked and redeems me from the plots and the plans of those whose intent is to destroy. No matter what the future may bring, God will be faithful to fortify me and never forget me.

Gary L. Leonard lives in Texas with his wife Connie. They have two grown children and two grandchildren. He has been a pastor for thirty-six years. He enjoys his three dogs, gardening, and wood working in his spare time.

Madison Penwell

From Spark to Fire

GOD HAS A great plan for each one of us—there's no doubt in my mind. But it's still difficult to know what exactly that plan is. Maybe you feel the Holy Spirit telling you to become a preacher, a youth minister, or a Christian doctor. We need followers of Jesus in every area.

I felt God transforming my passion for young people when I was ten years old, during my first mission trip to San Luis Potosi, Mexico. My great-grandparents started the children's home, Casa Hogar. My uncle now runs the home and has a wonderful passion for kids. On that first trip I remember thinking, "Man, I want to live here!" But I knew I was too young and immature.

I visited Casa Hogar every year with groups of families, a few friends, and soon, by myself. The passion continued to burn inside me. But I never thought it would be possible to live in Mexico. I've always figured that God's nudges were just feelings.

Yet each time I swing through the doors at Casa Hogar, my urge to be there increases. My last trip down, last spring, I had the chance to speak with my uncle. He asked me, "Madison, what do you want to do with your life?"

I was afraid to tell him I wanted to take his and his wife's spot when they got too old because he is very attached to his home. "Oh, I don't know yet," I said.

"You don't want to take over the home?"

I was surprised to hear this question from Uncle Juan, but it comforted me that he had the same plan I did.

We talked about how I would need to prepare myself. The more we talked, the scarier it got. My dream evolved into reality. God has great things in store!

We talked about the necessity of visiting as often as possible. I need to learn how to manage the budget and finances, cooking and cleaning needs, and simply how to run a children's home. I'm so excited to see where God will take me!

Transformed

The thing is, God's already put me on the journey. Ever since fifth grade, I've had a passion to start a young girls' Bible study—but it just wasn't possible. Even so, I let God prepare me over the next few years, allowing me to struggle with friends, boys, and self-hatred. Though my preteen years were difficult, I had no doubt God wanted to use these experiences to help other girls.

My freshman year was the first year I did my girls' Bible study for fifth and sixth graders. I became friends with them. They could feel how much I cared for them. Last year, I had a fifth- and sixth-grade Bible study on Wednesday nights, and another study for seventh- and eighth-graders on Sunday afternoons. It was hard to manage my time, but God helped me through. My experiences truly resonated with my girls.

I have always wanted an older girl to take me under her wing, anyone other than my mom. As much as I love her, it's not the same. Because I never had that, at least not yet, I am determined to be that for the girls in my church. I love that they feel comfortable telling me anything and know I will not judge them, but be an honest friend.

I'm so thankful God transformed my passion for mentoring girls from spark to fire. Now I know I can use it while I'm in Mexico. Although the language barrier is tough, I can share with them my struggles in the same way I have with my American girls.

I hope to use my experiences to, one day, write my own book. I'd love to go around the world as a teen and be a motivational speaker. I don't know if it's possible, but I believe that through God anything is possible, so hopefully a day will come when I can share my experiences in school, churches, or anywhere.

Madison Penwell is a seventeen-year-old writer from Michigan. She has an passion for young people and envisions running a home for children in San Luis Potosi, Mexico. She enjoys painting, sewing, playing piano, and beating boys on any sporting field.

Laura Krämer

Heart Exchange

HOT TEARS ESCAPED as I climbed on the treadmill. High expectations of distraction threatened reality. I was rejected. Even worse, *she* was accepted. It wasn't fair.

The more I ranted and raved, the more I obsessed. In this soul devouring game I played, I knew the bitter truth. I hated her. I not only detested that she was promoted, but I loathed everything about her. From her feminine frame and ease with fashion to her commitment to God, I couldn't stop fixating on the many petty ways I disdained her. Rage pumped through every part of my being. I felt the danger of it exploding through my skin.

Hoping to drown the chaos in my mind, I turned up my iPod to maximum levels. I was desperate for relief, yet too weary to pray. I chose to submit my crazed envy to moans and groans.

The music played on, as if God Himself orchestrated the playlist to create just the right soundtrack for the day's drama. I listened in as God's voice thundered ever so gently to the depths of my soul.

You feel jealousy raging within you. Beloved, this is how I feel towards you. I am jealous for you.

He had my attention. As much as He identified with my extreme emotions, I could not ignore His were holy. Gripping the sides of the treadmill, I closed my eyes and held on for more.

Your jealousy keeps Me from having all of you. I will not relent until I have completely captured every part of your heart. I am jealous for you.

My pace slowed as His words overwhelmed me. God's rebuke wrapped up in His crazy love for me. The music became a wild expression of His passionate pursuit to capture every part of my soul. He took the very emotion that overpowered me to demonstrate how captivated He was by me. Suppressing sobs, I heard His request.

Give Me your heart.

Transformed

My head spun. Response required forsaking all offenses. What would I do without my right to whine and complain? Was I brave enough to give in?

I became mysteriously enticed by the hope of freedom from hatred's grip. God-given courage welled up within me. It was time. Wiping away sweat and tears, I surrendered to the One who calls me beloved.

Lord, here's my heart.

Then the Lord took His turn in what was to be the great exchange. He placed within my chest His very own heart. His gift took my breath away.

I opened my eyes. Nothing had changed around me, yet everything was transformed within me. I was finally free. Free of me. Who would have thought that in this smelly, sweaty place God would give me His pure and holy heart?

Laura Krämer is a speaker, writer, and designer of The Psalm 23 Bracelet©. Featured in numerous national and local publications, her design has sold in over thirty-five nations. Laura's passion is leading others closer to the heart of God. She lives in Southern California with her husband and two boys. Visit her website and blog at www.LauraKramer.org.

Lyndie Blevins
God's Recital

"LYNDIE, TOMORROW IS Easter Sunday." Mom's seamstress' fingers caressed the texture of my new suit. "You're playing the piano for Easter church service?"

I leaned against the desk to steady myself. My stomach dropped like a falling elevator. The reality of the next day flooded my mind with painful memories of childhood recitals.

At my first recital, I was okay until I heard my name called. *Oh, no. My turn.* My eight-year-old heart pounded in my chest. Every eye in the sanctuary followed me to the stage. I saw how small I seemed in the black lacquer surface of the piano's grandeur. The stage was a lonesome place. Settling on the bench, I stretched my legs to the floor, but my feet couldn't reach the pedals.

Shudders crossed my shoulders as I carefully placed my fingers on the right keys to start my piece. Stillness saturated the audience. They were all waiting for me to play. My hands became heavy from their desires. My fingers stumbled through the piece, dashing my hopes of being an accomplished pianist.

Each year, I twirled in the new dress my mom made me until I remembered the coming recital. My beautiful dress promised beautiful music, which I knew I wouldn't deliver. So, somewhere in grade school, I decided playing the piano for an audience wasn't my gift. Funny thing is, I continued studying and enduring recitals into my high school years.

After college, my first major purchase was an old upright piano which wouldn't hold a tune. The perfect instrument for a bad piano player.

A quiet decade passed. One night, with a concordance and a parallel Bible open on my dining room table, while researching the theme of "God is love," these words jumped off the page at me, "No one has seen God at any time; if we love one another, God abides in us, and His love is perfected in us" (1 John 4:12 NASB). My body tingled. The words cut my heart. A wail rose from the soles of my feet. "Dear Lord, I never want anyone to say 'Where is God?' in my presence again."

My heart broke as I recalled memories of times people hadn't seen God in me.

I didn't understand what I prayed, but the Holy Spirit did. He heard my "groanings too deep for words" (Romans 8:26 NASB). He went to work building on the foundation of my salvation. I wish I could say I prayed this prayer and the next day I was a different person. That's not my story.

While my prayer was immediate, the Spirit's work has been slow and steady. He's creating a spirit of love in me. Not long after this prayer, God said to me, "Lyndie, it is time for you to play for people."

Someone invited me to play. The people were desperate for a piano player. They loved me even though I began by playing the melody with one hand, one note at a time. I practiced at home and in public. Yet, every missed or wrong note I played made me winch. As I persisted through the pain of facing my fears, I realized I projected my anguish onto the faces of those in my audience. After each performance, people hugged and encouraged me. Slowly, over a period of about eight years, my skills and confidence increased.

When my friend, Toby, an interim music leader, came to me during Wednesday dinner and asked if I would play at his church, I knew it was God asking. For four days, I practiced the songs he selected.

Sunday morning, I donned my beautiful new suit, packed my music and my fear, and headed for the church. The moment I walked through the door, the congregation accepted and embraced me. Men and women shared how much they appreciated me. As I played, each hymn filled me with joy. I wanted them to know and hear my love for God.

Lyndie Blevins lives in Duncanville, Texas, with two dogs and a cat. She shares her passion for senior adults as she cares for aging parents and her Sunday school class. Lyndie is currently working on stories about Sage, Texas. To learn more about her ministry or Sage, visit her website www.guidingwind.com.

Carolyn Stanford Goss

God Loves Lefties Too

"YOU CAN'T RENEW this book," whispered the librarian in the Glendale, Arizona, Public Library. "Other girls want to read it, too."

I whispered meekly back, "OK." I was eleven years old. I was shy and skinny. I already wore a size eight shoe, which made me prone to bumping into things. My short black hair curled in every direction. My teeth looked as if the tooth fairy had lost her sense of direction and had thrown my teeth in at random, so that some were nearly on top of each other. A southpaw, I held my pencil upside down as left-handed people often do, and having to write so awkwardly gave me one more reason to feel self-conscious.

I placed *Anne of Green Gables* on the polished blonde wood counter. As the librarian checked the book in and slipped the card into the pocket inside the back cover I hesitated. I so wanted to walk the green fields of Avonlea again! But I couldn't get up the nerve to ask her to allow me to renew the book, so as she put it on the reshelving cart, I turned around and went into the children's library to discover my next great read.

That summer I spent my days reading, propped up on a red brick ledge attached to our house. The overhang above it provided some shade against the blast furnace that we called summer in Arizona. Sitting there I'd disappear into another time and another place. As the afternoon passed I didn't notice the heat much—I was gone, walking with Anne Shirley around the Lake of Shining Waters, sprawling on the rag rug in the March family's living room as Jo grumbled about not having Christmas presents, or holding my blind sister Mary's hand as we ran across the waving prairie grass. In late afternoon my mom would stick her head out the front door and announce, "Come on, Miss Bookworm, dinner's ready." Kids at school used that nickname to tease me, but I wore it as a badge of honor, and I knew my mom, a book lover like me, meant it as one.

I'd probably win the library's summer reading contest again, but that wasn't why I read so many books. I read because I could "be" another person besides the gawky, awkward adolescent I was. As I sat barefooted in the yellow or pink sailcloth shorts and halter top my mother had whipped up for me, I could imagine myself dressed in white stockings and pinafore or corseted into a long dove-gray dress with mother-of-pearl buttons down the front. I could trudge through snow or lollygag in a birch bark canoe on a golden autumn afternoon. I could be smart, beautiful, and popular. And, I could have long, *straight* hair. I could look like anyone but me.

It wasn't that I hated myself. I just wasn't satisfied with my looks. During that summer I had begun to feel uncomfortable in my own skin. It took me a few years to admit something: much I as loved books, and I still do, those imaginary places and people were temporary escapes from Carolyn. Exciting as my transformation was, it never lasted once I closed the book.

Then in college I became acquainted with a young woman who had stringy hair, a bad complexion, and the sunniest smile I had ever encountered. Her life exemplified a transformation that had made her beautiful from the inside out. I remembered something from the Bible I had heard before but had not understood: "If anyone is in Christ, the new creation has come: The old has gone, the new is here!"

I decided I could be like her. I slowly learned to accept myself and to see my quirks as one-of-a-kind gifts from God. I learned to laugh about them, and eventually I even learned they could be strengths. Even my love of words on paper, yet another thing many other kids thought was weird about me, has served me well.

I'm not going to say that being a lefty, being a klutz, or having unmanageable hair are characteristics I'd wish for. But I know now God can use every detail of our DNA map if we allow him to transform us from within. The bodies he designed for us may look the same, but we're not the same inside. And inside is where it counts.

Carolyn Stanford Goss is a partner with her husband Leonard G. Goss in GoodEditors.com, an editorial services and ghostwriting firm. They are the authors of the *Little Style Guide to Great Christian Writing and Publishing*.

Carole Klock

From Victim to Victor

THE ONLY CERTAINTIES in life are death and taxes. I suggest adding a third item to this list: transition. Our lives are constantly in flux; we are presently going through transition or we have just been through one. If neither of these scenarios apply, we're probably about to enter a time of change.

Life begins with an explosive transition when the new life leaves the safety, comfort, and warmth of the womb to enter a world of noise, bright lights, and chattering voices. From this shocking beginning, the little one embarks on a journey of constant change that lasts well into adulthood.

My father walked away when I was two. A year later, my mother placed my brother and me in foster care, and we were sent to separate homes. I lived in five different foster homes the first year until I was finally placed in a home where I remained for the next fourteen years. This was not an ideal situation, as while there I experienced mental, emotional, physical, and sexual abuse.

I struggled to measure up to expectations; no matter how I tried, I was never good enough. "You can't do anything right! You lie all the time. I have never seen such a bad kid!" my foster mother constantly reminded me. I believed her angry words. I had a talent for getting into trouble, although I didn't do it on purpose. My foster mother was certain I had a mean streak. She accused me of plotting and planning ways to be disobedient. "Get out of my sight! Go to your room and think about what you did wrong."

Deep inside lived the hope that life would get better someday. I prayed hard, even though I didn't know to whom I was praying. I only knew there had to be Someone out there somewhere. Thankfully, there was.

One day, when I was about six, I found myself sitting on my bed, dejected and sobbing, when someone spoke to me. No one else was in the room, yet I heard a voice. That voice was

145

so real I got down and looked underneath my bed. When I found no one, I crossed the room and looked in my closet. No one was there.

The Voice was kind, gentle, and comforting. He said, "I'm here; it's all right." In the next few years the Voice spoke to me several times. "Someday I will make it all better. I will turn your upside-down life right-side up." I did not know His name, but I believed His promise.

I accepted Christ as my Savior at the age of fifteen. I heard the Voice again. Even though He'd been silent for several years, I recognized the voice of my Savior. Now my Friend had a name, the Name Above all Names.

I met my future husband when I was eighteen. "That boy just wants one thing," my angry foster mother warned when the relationship grew serious between us. "You don't know what you're doing. I think it is time you went to live with your real mother."

I moved in with my mother and brother for six weeks before I married, and it was a precious time for all of us. My brother Bill and I had always held a strong bond, even though we had not seen each other often. Mother and I became great friends. I asked all the hard questions and she answered them all.

Many years have passed since then. My husband had a successful career in the Marine Corps. We have raised three wonderful children and we have seven grandchildren and two great grandchildren. The relationship between my mother and me deepened over the years, and she lived to be eighty-two.

There are times in our lives when transition leads to transformation. Today joy fills my life, and I love singing praises to my Lord and Savior. The promises He gave me have been fulfilled, and my earthly transformation from victim to victor is complete.

In the future a home awaits me with Jesus my Lord. Then my eternal transformation will be complete.

Carole Klock was raised in foster care and accepted Christ at age fifteen. She was co-editor of her high school newspaper and is now part of a writer's group in Colorado Springs. Her passions include family, writing, music, Miniature Schnauzers, and quilting.

Jennings Riley

Through Tinted Lenses

L ITTLE DID I know the magnitude of the transformation God would work in my life when my family set out for Uganda on November 15, 2009. It was the first time we had been out of the country as a family. We were barely nine hours into the trip when things took a nosedive. After the flight was delayed we only had twenty minutes to change planes. My father was the last to get through screening, and before he had time to put his shoes back on we were running. Wide-eyed and winded, we reached the flight attendant at our gate who, with a slight twinkle in her eye and a smile playing on her lips, welcomed us aboard. Turns out we were the last to board and our luggage was still on the other plane. But we were there. We thought we had seen the worst.

The first week or so we spent with the Sivages, missionaries teaching at Uganda Baptist Seminary (UBS). Originally we were supposed to stay on the campus of the seminary where my father was teaching, but the apartment we were to stay in had flooded. Our luggage was stuck in London. Even so, the Lord worked all things together for good, using that time to knit our relationship with the Sivages.

The greatest time of fear for my mother came next when my younger brother, Rhett, began to look puffy. He continued to swell, becoming almost unrecognizable. To my mother's great dismay, the doctor was out of the country, but providentially one of the other missionaries, Harry, was a pharmacist. Harry came to our now dry apartment to check on Rhett. When he came through the mosquito net that we used for a door during the day, he had an even more jovial expression than normal. He had managed to procure some prednisone, a steroid that would reduce Rhett's swelling. Our first couple of weeks in Uganda were, by our standards, rocky. As a stress reliever, we arranged to take a three-day safari. After returning, we settled into life in Uganda.

Transformed

Compared to the sufferings of the people of Uganda, particularly those students who sacrificed so much to have access to theological education, our troubles are beyond trivial. Most students at UBS have to ride overcrowded vans with the ever-present threat of sickness and theft. After twenty years of brutal civil war and total devastation, students from the northern part of Uganda find it particularly difficult to attend seminary. They take time out of rebuilding communities, families, and homes to receive theological education to be further equipped to meet the spiritual needs of their community.

Each term at UBS lasts three weeks. The first week the majority of the students are suffering from malaria. By the second week the medical staff at the seminary has treated them, and the students are relatively healthy. However, by the third week the students, who live in bunkhouses, have passed around whatever other ailments they brought with them. But joy bursts from within. How could they have such joy?

"Through all their troubles," one Ugandan pastor says, "even those most affected by war in the north over the last twenty years are happy. They are happy to know Christ Jesus, to now have peace, and to be able to go home and rebuild their lives and churches." Our time and conversation with students were always punctuated with smiles and laughter. We never heard a complaint from the students. They took seriously the Psalmist's admonition that this is the Lord's day and we should rejoice and be glad in it. (Psalm 118:24) One student showed how committed he was to being equipped for ministry. When his father died on the first day of the term, he missed only one day of class.

Before going to Africa I knew that people suffered much more than I, but I did not comprehend the magnitude of their suffering nor the joy they experienced in it. Even now that I have seen their faith and joy in the storm, it is still difficult to grasp. Until you see firsthand that kind of faith, it is nearly impossible to understand.

My view of suffering was having to do extra chores around the house, wearing a tie, and going to a conference I didn't see the value of attending. Now I understand how utterly and inexcusably pathetic my view of suffering was. Things I used to consider trials have become trivial. Although I still have to relearn the same lesson over and over again, I find myself struggling with it less and less. I have made it my goal to see things through the tinted lens of a UBS student.

William Jennings Bryan Riley II enjoys jumping from world to world and dying a thousand times and then living again. When Jennings is not in an alternate reality, he can be found in New Orleans, Louisiana, where he lives with his family and a little white fluffball.

148

Dana Rausch

Extreme Makeover - Home Edition

T HE FIRST TIME I visited Bill, an 89-year-old blind man, he asked me to write a note for him. As I pulled an index card from the desk drawer, a cockroach crawled across my hand. Although he was unaware of his filthy surroundings, I knew Bill's mobile home was in need of an extreme makeover.

At first, we visited every few months, then monthly, then weekly, then daily, making sure he had food, help with laundry, and dispensing his medication. Because he was blind, I wrote checks for him to sign. He didn't have any family, so he became part of ours.

Eventually, Bill agreed to some changes. While he was at a doctor's appointment, the makeover began. Workers removed furniture, pulled up old flooring, and every surface was cleaned. A broken toilet was replaced, the garbage disposal repaired, cabinet door hinges fixed, and brand new flooring installed throughout. The new floor was down and the furniture back in four hours! He came home and said, "It sure smells good."

Bill's renovation caused me to contemplate makeover parallels, steps necessary when families encounter difficult situations.

No amount of bleach, scrubbing, or scrapers could remove the build-up of grime and neglect on the floor. The only solution was to remove and replace the flooring. A family is often in the same predicament. No amount of re-hashing will fix the problem. We need to agree to toss out the hurt and loss and begin with a new resolve. Just as Bill's home took on a fresh new look, so we should change our outlook.

Neglect allowed cobwebs to accumulate. Vacuuming eliminated evidence of neglect. Families also allow cobwebs to gather—preconceived ideas, assumptions, and hurts. If they appear, they need to be addressed or removed.

The toilet wobbled, but it was not obvious why. A serious problem seen only when it was detached, the floor underneath had eroded. A metal flange was placed on top of the damaged floor, and a new toilet installed.

Families may have unseen broken places. Trying to fix problems we perceive in others is futile, but we can allow the Lord to show us our own part in the issue. Much like we could not ignore the problem with the toilet, we must observe brokenness and deal with it.

Someone had scooted the kitchen table across the new floor. A sharp piece of wood protruded from a chair leg and gouged the new flooring. The beautiful floor makeover was now clearly damaged. The contractor put glue behind the flap, massaged it until it fit so the gouge disappeared.

Families may experience a gouge now and then. A choice must be made to either throw a fit and rant, "everything is ruined," or let Jesus be the glue that binds you back together. Then give the glue time to adhere and fix gouges.

Thin plywood cabinets throughout the home had numerous broken hinges. New cabinets were preferable, but not possible. Making the best of it, the cabinets were painted and hardware was replaced. The family you were born into was never a mistake. At times a new one is preferred, but not possible. Take what you have and make the best of it. We can't start with a new family, so think of them as "Cash in the Attic," and consider them valuable.

Take the time and effort to transform family relationships. Fix broken places with forgiveness and by learning to let things go. Decide to restore your relationships. Romans 12:2 says, "Do not conform any longer to the pattern of this world, but be transformed by the renewing of your mind."

Any house can be renovated, but often families need an "Extreme Makeover-Home Edition."

Dana Rausch has been married thirty-one years, has three adult children, and twenty years experience in women's ministry. She is a women's retreat speaker and Bible study leader, with the ability to bring God's Word alive through her gift of applicable picture stories.

Connie Payne

Where am I, God?

IT'S SO DARK…I can't see anything. I want to sit up but I feel so weak… something is happening. I'm being rocked gently.

Is that you, God?

I've never been this relaxed. I could sleep forever. What are these images? Memories? I haven't thought about some of these things for a long time.

Ah, my beautiful daughters. Three very different beings. Three very different lives. They reflect me—my journey. God, mend the hurt that I've caused. I was able to give birth, but had no idea how to be a mom.

I always had men around. You knew what I really wanted, God. I needed the attention of my father but my father was a busy man. It was fun being the center of attention, though. Parties were a blast—I was always the one drinking and dancing on the tables. Wow, I see this clearly, yet the men are faceless. God, only you know who Carrie's father is. I was an alcoholic and a crack addict. And selfish. I dragged my sweet little girl to every party I could; she slept in places I'll never remember. She watched me—the things I did—and made them her own. It's my fault Carrie's an addict.

Watch over her, God. Help her to be a better mom than I was.

Annie is smiling at me. She looks like her father. Thank you, God. He was there when I was out partying and getting high. I wanted so badly for our marriage to last, but now I know it was a blessing he took Annie and left. I hate that she didn't have her mother. Please forgive me, Father, for the pain I caused.

I can see Becca's face. She has my eyes. She also has a smile that melts my heart. I wanted to make things better for her, God. You know when I inherited the money, I planned to make life good for my girls.

Why couldn't I stop myself?

I paid for the best babysitters, bought expensive clothes, gave money for entertainment—things any girl would love—while hosting all-night parties with food, beer, and drugs for everyone.

I know now, God, it was you who orchestrated this. Annie came to pick me up. The money was gone and I'd been kicked out of the crack-house. She opened the car door and said nothing. There was nothing to say. Next thing I know, we're pulling up to a red brick building.

What's this?

She broke the silence, "I can't do anything else for you, Mom. Get out." I sat there. Empty. I had absolutely nothing left inside. I got out and walked up to the door. The door of a homeless shelter.

God, you loved me at my lowest point. You saw something in me and waited. The door opened and I asked for a room. After being told I'd have a curfew, I stomped out yelling, "No one has ever told me when to be in at night, and I'm not about to let you start!" I walked to the end of the sidewalk and stopped. You must have had a sense of humor, God, seeing me puffed up like that—thinking my rights were violated. As I stood there for that moment, I heard you loud and clear.

Every decision you've ever made in your life has been wrong. Are you ready to listen to someone else?

Suddenly, I saw every bad choice and the suffering I caused.

It wasn't easy seeing what I'd done. Or what I had become. But, it turned out to be my beginning. I went back and moved in that night. I learned about you, God. At first I didn't understand your love—because I'd been loved in many positions—but it became real. After years of living life my way and taking things into my own hands, I gave it to you. And my life has never been the same.

Looking back now, God, it's hard to believe how much has changed. It's amazing to have Becca with me again; I'm content being single; and I'm thrilled to speak to hundreds of teens about the new life you've given to me. I never thought it could be this good.

Lying here, I feel myself fading. Am I going home? Are the drugs demanding their final payment? Please, Lord, if you are taking me home, watch over my daughters and my grandchildren.

Bring them home safely.

This story is dedicated to Lou Adams who died of a grand mal seizure in 2003 after years of drug use.

Connie Payne is the Director of Communications at Inner City Mission of Springfield, Illinois, and has been writing locally for over ten years. She and her husband have six children and two grandchildren.

Sharon Baijense

Inside Out

"SHARON, LET'S GO for a hike with the kids."

I sighed. "No, I don't want to go; you take them and have a good time."

"Are you sure?" I could see he wanted me to come with them.

"I want some 'me time.' You go have fun."

My husband often invited me to go hiking with him and the kids, but I didn't want to slow them down. They would need to take extra breaks for me to catch up with them, or end the hike early. No way was I going to swim, get on a bike, or horse. I told myself I didn't want to join them when I really did want to go. It was difficult to see the pictures that were taken of fun they had without me. Today that is no longer the case. I now initiate the swimming, hiking, biking, walking, and most any outdoor activity. My secret reason for avoiding activities with my family was my excess weight.

Transformation involves upheaval. Change needs to come from the inside out to be effective. It can be messy. We need to be moldable for Christ and His will for our lives. We don't get to choose when He is in control and when we are in control. The focus needs to be on Him and His will for our lives. How do we hear His will if we have garbage on the inside? First, we have to be willing to get rid of the garbage that is in *His* place. Then He can have His special place in our lives. I know this is not an easy thing to do. When I first started cleaning out my garbage, it was uncomfortable. It also took several years for me to realize my ultimate goal. Only with God's tender guidance and constant assistance was I able to let God change me.

As a mom with a husband and four young kids it became difficult for me to keep up with them and all of their activities. I needed to lose a lot of weight. Before I could focus on losing weight I had to redirect my mindset. Doing this can take time, but when I refocused I was able to move forward. Yes, our garbage likes to creep back into place. Our job is to keep enough focus on not letting it back in.

This process took me a full two years to achieve a healthy weight. Yes, the changes came at a slow pace, but a steady one. Baby steps made all the difference for me. When I make a change I think in baby steps. They seem more attainable. I am able to manage them one by one. When I think about making a food substitution, it's in small unnoticeable amounts. For example, I made a moderate change from whole milk to 1% milk. When I started, I used half whole milk and half 2% milk. Soon after that it was just 2% milk. I went through the same process when I switched to 1% milk. I listened to my body and made sure that I was comfortable with the changes before moving on. I had to be gentle rather than pushy with myself. One of the most disciplined people in the world, the Apostle Paul advised us, "Let your gentleness be evident to all" (Philippians 4:5 NIV).

What a difference this has made in my life for my family. We are now able to enjoy many activities together since the removal of my stumbling block. I no longer lie to myself and I don't miss out on the fun. I am excited and eager to join my family in activities. I no longer sit on the sidelines watching my children; I am making memories with them.

Sharon Baijense has a heart for women struggling with weight loss. She knows the pain and discouragement of this battle through personal experience. She's a dynamic speaker full of humor and honest truth. Sharon gives women guidance and direction to succeed through discipline and lifestyle change. Contact Sharon at hsbaijense@aol.com

Cyn Rogalski

Dreamweaver

MY DREAM OF someday writing a book began in 2004. My son was in his last year of high school and no longer needed his stay-at-home mom running his life. I needed something to fill the void. I contacted an author I enjoyed reading and asked how to get started. She sent me a long list of resources by e-mail and wished me well. At the top of the list was the *Christian Writer's Market Guide*. I bought one and left it near the computer so it would be handy to pick up and access information when I had a few minutes. I was ready to start writing. Piece of cake.

Imagine my surprise when I found it nearly impossible to write more than three sentences in three years. I would sit at the computer and stare at the screen, write a few words, delete them, write a sentence, and delete that. Writing is hard work. I had no idea how people could possibly succeed in this field. My writing dream got wedged into Sally's book and put back on the "dream" shelf. I occasionally looked at it longingly, sighed, and then continued my life. This went on for three more years. A maniacal need to clean up and de-clutter caused me to pick up Sally's book again. In it, I had placed a CLASS flyer received from a friend. On a whim, I looked up the website. The memory of my last attempt at writing came to mind. Can I do this? I asked myself. I heard the Lord say "No. But I can."

Encouraged, I looked at the website and began to get excited when I saw all the different programs offered. A one-day writing seminar was to be held in a nearby city. It would necessitate a two-night stay-over, but would be affordable. I went, was hooked, and began to think of myself as a writer. I started looking at things around me through a writer's eyes. I attended a weeklong conference to better my writing skills. I knew I was doing what God called me to do, rather than just filling a void.

Returning home, I was fired up with new energy to write. After a month or two, the excitement waned. I couldn't understand what was happening. I had prayer partners, praying for my newfound ministry. I was making time to write around my full time job. I was doing all the things I knew to keep this dream alive. I desperately sought the Lord for direction but received no answer. My writing time dwindled. Personal worship suffered. I felt powerless to escape this downward spiral. I knew I needed to get out of this desert place, but everything seemed to fail. Unbeknownst to me, the Lord was preparing me for the next step I would need to take. I had been at the same church for a number of years, and my attendance had become sporadic, the worship rote. I was conformed to the status quo, but the seeds that were planted at the first seminar were ready to germinate, and they were not in good soil. God was renewing my mind, and He was stretching me to get me to where He needed me to be.

A women's conference was being held at a nearby church. I went seeking His direction and affirmation. I was blessed by this conference. God gently, but firmly, led me to a different church where I experienced a burst of Holy Spirit fire in my worship and devotional time. Today I find myself surrounded by people who are as excited as I am to see what God is doing in my life. Every day brings new joy as I find myself filled with new hope, energy, and focus to accomplish what He has planned for me to do. I found that the transformation happens when we stop resisting the Holy Spirit and allow His leading. I have been renewed indeed.

Cyn Rogalski is a sculptress, author, and speaker. Her biblically-based sculptures are the basis for her speaking ministry, "ArtFully Yours." Cyn has been published in CLASS publications and on-line. Her blog, "Still Water and Ponderings," can be viewed on her website, www.cynrogalski.com, where she writes whatever God chooses.

Ginger Cox

Divine Dialogue

GOOD MORNING, LORD. I humbly come to You, not liking who I am. (Look at me correcting myself, even in my prayer journal. I'm convinced there is no human cure for perfectionism, especially in melancholies!)

"Father, You know I am disappointed about not winning the book cover photo contest. I was delighted a friend got honorable mention, and I'm happy for the winner, but I have this innate need to have my efforts valued. Do I really crave recognition of my worth? I'm ashamed.

"Lord, when I got the email announcing the winner last night, I was tired from working on a query letter and book proposal all day. I know writers must expect rejections. Katherine Stockett received sixty rejections before *The Help* was published, but I crumble with a single rejection. I know Scripture says we are to persist with worthy projects, but I question the worthiness of the results of my projects. I seem to focus on feel-good moments. Are my spiritual growth presentations and writing truly worthy, or am I self-absorbed? Am I my worst enemy?

"Father, I know You want me to stand strong and persevere in what is good, and here I sit whining. Please forgive my selfish focus, once again, and transform my attitude to match Your will. Renew my mind. Help me move beyond this depression. Please lift me up, Lord. Make me useful in Your kingdom. Amen."

Pushing aside my prayer journal, I turn to the daily devotionals. I know from past experience that God often speaks to me more poignantly after I honestly lay my concerns before Him. I open the Bible and a handful of devotional books, seeking His response in at least one of them.

Transformed

I open *Our Daily Bread* and read the reference, Luke 19:37-44. Before Jesus' triumphal entry into Jerusalem, the disciples praised God. Yet, prior to that, Jesus wept (v. 41). Seeing Jesus despondent, even after others praised God, shows me He relates to emotional whirlwinds that swirl high and low. Thank You, Lord, for this insight.

Then, I turn to the third chapter of 1 Samuel, referenced in *Open Windows*. When God first called the boy during the night, Samuel didn't know who was calling. A second time God called Samuel. Although he was eager to please, Samuel didn't know how. When God spoke a third time, Samuel acknowledged God's call, listened to Him, and obeyed, despite his fear. This reminds me my true need is to give God my full attention, respond "Speak, Lord, for Thy servant is listening," and obey.

Looking at the *Turning Points* devotional, I read Psalm 85, a prayer of revival. Once again, Scripture echoes my self-centered concerns regarding worth and validation, and His answer is clear. "Wilt Thou not Thyself revive us again, that Thy people may rejoice in Thee?" (v. 6). Yes, Father, I need reviving. "Righteousness will go before Him, and will make His footsteps into a way" (v. 13). I know this Old Testament passage points to Christ, the Righteous One, who made the way for me to follow.

Finally, I turn to *Jesus Calling* by Sarah Young, who regularly reveals the compassionate, loving care of Christ. Today's reading includes: "A refreshed, revitalized mind is able to sort out what is important and what is not. In its natural condition, your mind easily gets stuck in trivial matters…. Communicate with Me continually, and I will put My thoughts into your mind." Young reminds me the transformation I want is available when I abide and commune with Jesus. I seek His thoughts and ways to replace my own.

I pull out my prayer journal again and continue writing: Lord, what a perfect red-letter day! Every single devotional spoke to my concerns. Thank You for transforming my pathetic self-absorption into a praise and worship time. Today's early morning AA (attitude adjustment) may be over, but I know our conversation will continue throughout the day and forever more.

Ginger Cox, a former public school educator, devotes her time to writing, inspirational presentations, and photography. She developed WRAP (Spiritual R&R Enrichment) sessions, written for a variety of educational and Christian publications, and created greeting cards with her nature photography. She shares a website with her husband at www.CoxWorks.com.

Kathy Keicher

Contracts

THE MORTGAGE PAYMENT was late. I was angry with my husband and felt all the pressure was on me. A neighbor suggested I contact Social Services for counseling. After all, it was free.

I called Social Services and scheduled an appointment. Hopeful, I rushed in to meet the person who might help me retrieve some balance.

Upon arrival, Mrs. Flock came around from her desk, took my hand in a warm embrace and said, "How are you doing today?"

Hope surged and my sense of desperation subsided as I sat down to talk with Mrs. Flock. She explained how her job worked within the system and handed me a form. "Please fill this out," she said. "So, tell me, how long has mental illness been in your family?"

"What?"

"Mental illness," drawing out the syllables as if I was slow in the head, "How long has mental illness been in your family?"

"There is no mental illness in my family!" I said, holding back as much anger as I could.

"Okay," she said. She nodded as though to say, yes there is.

"I know I've been beaten down, I know life has been difficult, but I'm not crazy!" Without another word, I quickly gathered my belongings and darted out of her office, enraged that she accused me of being mentally ill. What a total waste of time.

I was back to square one.

Mrs. Flock's question demoralized an already bewildered woman. I wasn't nuts. I rejected her words. I was weakened by issues in my life. I was not going to add her label to my list of hardships. I had to shake that off.

Transformed

As if life wasn't hard enough, my husband called to say he was not coming home, ever. My daughter and I were on our own, I thought. How were we going to make it with no money and no job prospects? I felt so betrayed.

On a cold January evening, we ran out of heat. Thumbing my last $25, I picked up the phone.

"Can you please come out?" I begged, "I have a three-year-old, and we're freezing." Begging was a new low in my life, but I was out of options.

Later that evening as the house warmed, I leafed through the Bible and the words of the Gospel of John leaped off the pages. Compelled to rededicate my life to Jesus, I cried out, "Lord, please fix my life. I promise to attend church every Sunday for the rest of my life."

Having fallen into the habit of not attending church, this promise was a sacrifice on my part. But I began to hold up my end of this new contract on the following Sunday. I was desperate and believed He would fix it all.

He began to transform my life immediately. I was hired to a new job, rented our house, and moved to an apartment closer to the new job, family, and friends. I enrolled my daughter in a local Montessori school. With renewed hope, I found my balance.

God fixed my life and I am grateful.

Even though my marriage contract failed, thirty-four years later, my contract with the Lord remains strong. He brought me to a higher plane than I had ever been. While there have been tough times, I have always had hope. Transformed!

After twenty years of corporate life, Kathy Keicher developed a string of retail stores. Coming to know the Lord powerfully, her value system changed. A Licensed Minister with a Master's degree in Bible, she serves in missions, hospital pastoral care, and local churches. Kathy, her husband, kids, and grands live in New Jersey.

PJ Gover

The Moment

TOWARD THE END of my high school years, I struggled to end a four and a half year abusive relationship.

My mother, older sister, and I were devastated by the sudden death of my beloved father in a car accident. After Daddy's death, we stopped going to church regularly. I tried to continue to pray and read the Bible. But in my pain and immaturity, I mistakenly filled the void left by my father's death with a dangerous person. I was ripe for exploitation.

I began breaking away at seventeen. Throughout those months, the abuser approached the house night after night, knocking on my bedroom window in order to bring torment and terror. It was his attempt to coerce me to reenter the relationship. By this time, I was so determined to stop the emotional and physical trauma that I would have rather died than endure further contact.

One night, as I heard the incessant raps, I sobbed uncontrollably out of anguish and utter hopelessness. I was not reading the Bible, quoting Scripture, praying, or seeking God. In fact, those were the furthest things from my mind.

However, God had other plans.

Out of nowhere, John 3:16, memorized years earlier in a children's class at church, pierced my mind and heart. So profound and startling, I immediately stopped crying, sat upright with full attention, and focused on the words so ingrained in my memory, "For God so loved the world that He gave His only begotten Son, that whosoever believeth in Him should not perish but have everlasting life" (KJV). It was as if I'd never heard this verse before. I realized in that moment I was perishing, not eternally, but perishing physically within the abusive relationship. Fear left. A gentle calmness enveloped me as I realized God's great protection for me in Jesus Christ.

I knew I didn't have to perish at the hands of anyone. I was a believer, a child of God Almighty. I grasped that God loved me. His love is unconditional and beyond my comprehension. No one could steal that. I knew I would endure and survive.

In college, I returned to consistent church attendance and lived my Christian beliefs. That very conscious and deliberate decision put me on the journey of spiritual growth. I now have a loving Christian husband, daughter, family, and friends.

Has my path been smooth? Has all sorrow disappeared? Have traumatic memories dissolved? No. I bear scars, not open wounds. God healed those. Even though chronic pain, health challenges, invasive surgeries, and blinding fatigue cloud my days, I remain steadfast on life's tumultuous ride.

I have no doubt God is real.

God's Word still comforts me. "Yea, though I walk through the valley of the shadow of death, I fear no evil; for Thou art with me" (Psalm 23:4 KJV). I've lived in valleys which can neither be jumped nor skirted around. Where valleys exist, mountains reside, and hope abounds. God's presence sustains me as I walk both.

God's Word still pierces my heart. "The word of God is living and active and sharper than any two-edged sword" (Hebrews 4:12 NASB). My heart needs guidance and instruction from the Word of a loving and compassionate God.

God's Word still changes me. "Do not be conformed to this world, but be transformed" (Romans 12:2 NASB). When I heed His Word and walk in His ways, He uses me and grows me thought by thought, choice by choice and, yes, moment by moment.

Each situation, each decision, each trial, each joy, each person I encounter afford opportunity and challenge for more amazing moments of transformation by the hand and Word of God.

No perishing for me, ever. "Thank you, Lord."

PJ Gover has taught the Bible for thirty-four years. She gains spiritual insights for health challenges and chronic pain. PJ earned a B.S. in Family Relations with a Psychology minor from Texas Tech University. She resides in Texas with her husband where she maintains a devotional ministry and blogs. www.citygirlgoincountry.com

Susan Lugli

The Reflection in the Mirror

I LAY ON my back staring at the ceiling. It was midnight, and shadows from the nurses' station danced through the glass door of my room. I heard the beeping machines around me. The stench of the raw, burned skin under my bandages was sickening. I had been in a major motor home fire and I had burns on 48% of my body. My back was shattered. Within seconds, my life changed. My husband, who was in the accident with me, had a slim chance of surviving. His room was two doors down from mine, close, yet far.

Each night was like the night before, lying and waiting for the nurse to come in and hurt me with the dreaded two-hour bandage change. Depression and anxiety dominated my emotions. Nights were the worst. Unable to move, and unable to sleep, my mind was overwhelmed with hopelessness.

One night, I held the call button in my hand, but was hesitant to bother the nurses. I needed to talk to someone, but the burn unit is a busy place. However, my emotional needs won the battle and I rang. Joan, one of the night nurses, immediately answered my call. I was elated to see her. She called me her prized patient and always listened when time permitted.

"What's going on with you tonight? Are you in pain? Why aren't you asleep?"

"Asleep" was a post-traumatic trigger word for me. I was asleep when the accident occurred, so I rarely slept now. Although irrational, I thought the accident would not have happened if I had been awake. In my drug-induced stupor, I felt a need to be on night duty, so someone could be in control. A person cannot live through such a traumatic event and not be changed. My pain was constant, regardless of medication. Then, fear set in.

As Joan stood in front of me, her pretty gold earrings caught my eye. In that moment, I shared my fear of looking like a monster.

"Will anyone accept the way I look now?"

Transformed

Joan pulled a chair to the bedside and listened. "Will I ever be normal again, or pretty, or able to walk? Will this pain ever go away? Will I be able to feed myself and wear pretty earrings again?"

Abruptly, Joan stopped me. "Have you looked at your face yet?"

"No, I'm afraid to."

She hopped up and left the room. I feared what would happen next.

Joan reentered the room with a mirror in her hand.

"No! I am afraid to look!" I had seen my arms and legs during the bandages changes, and I looked like a freak.

She came closer and brushed my hair, saying quietly, "You are pretty. Your face is all right. It is rosy with first-degree burns that will go away."

She took her earrings off and gently clipped them onto my ears. As I wept, I mustered the courage to look at my reflection in the mirror. For five long weeks, I'd worried about my appearance. Now, with the help of a compassionate nurse and a simple mirror, fear transformed into relief.

Since the time of the accident, I've been through many transformations, and I'm grateful for those who gently ushered me into this new, unplanned life. It has been a long process with many changes, but I am who I am today because of this hard journey.

Susan Lugli is a Christian speaker and author. Her stories have been published in *Chicken Soup for the Christian Woman's Soul, Chicken Soup for the Caregiver's Soul, Today's Christian Woman* magazine and many others. She is an advocate for burn survivors and speaks on their behalf. E-mail her at: suenrusty@aol.com

Danni Andrew

When God Closes a Door, He Opens a Window!

"…I will … open for you the windows of heaven and pour out for you a blessing until it overflows."

—Malachi 3:10

TAKING CARE OF my aging mother with little help from siblings left me feeling like I was a little girl standing in the rain, soaked to the skin and terrified. She was found unconscious and rushed to the hospital. Her body temperature was dangerously low. Doctors and nurses rushed to her side and worked to bring her back to us. Six long hours later she finally woke up.

"I just want to be left alone and in peace!" My mother's words were emphatic, and I wondered if we should have heeded her words. As I left her room that day I had no idea I would have to stand, alone and afraid, between her and the rest of my family.

Mom had a stroke while in the hospital, which left her unable to speak or swallow well. When she became stable enough to leave the Intensive Care Unit, she was transferred to a nursing home.

"Take her to the emergency room; maybe they can run some tests and do something!" my family demanded. She kept pulling the feeding tube out of her nose, and the fourth time she refused to let them put it back in. Her words echoed in my mind and I knew she didn't want to live like this.

"If she wants to eat, feed her," I told the nurses. "If she wants to get out of bed, get her up. Whatever she wants to do, let her do it." The words hurt me as I said them, but I knew she only wanted peace and quiet in her final days.

"Killer! Killer!" rang in my ears as I endured threats and angry words from my family because of this decision. It only made me more determined to allow her the dignity to pass from this world peacefully and on her own terms.

Transformed

Mom finally went to sleep on July 31, 2011. I had done what I promised her I would do; I took care of her until the day she died, and then I buried her properly. Giving up Mom was one of the hardest things I have ever done. In my prayers I told God that I would turn my heart, my soul, my body, and everything about my life over to Him. That meant giving God everything, even if it meant my mother and best friend!

Like a child holding her favorite toy behind her back, I reluctantly relented and handed him my whole life. With the passing of my mother I let go of the hurt and pain of my childhood, the years and tears that had kept me down as an adult. The rain that had covered my life finally cleared and I stood on top of a mountain, looking at the sun as it rose and feeling the Holy Spirit everywhere.

I can finally see a bit of what is ahead. When doubt creeps in I know it is the enemy still trying to trip me up, but what God has planned is far better than anything I could ever come up with. His way is better than my way, and I am determined to walk in it.

Whatever God asks of me I will do. Whatever God tells me to say I will say, and whatever God directs me to do, I will do. The sun is up and His glory is flooding my world. The time has come to march out onto the battlefield and face the calling head on, so I will look out the window, step out of the shadows, and embrace that which God has set before me.

Danni Andrew has lived in the Four Corners area of New Mexico for forty years, after moving from Washington State. She has three grown children and five grandchildren. She teaches Home Economics part time, writes, oil paints, and coordinates costumes for an interdenominational passion play.

Andrea Brown

Rebirth

IF YOU SEE my smiling face, you know that it is positive." That's what I told my husband before he left for work. Later, when I surprised him at his office, I wore a smile.

I couldn't wait to tell everyone the news of my pregnancy. Especially my mother, who recently battled breast cancer.

Aside from occasional nausea, I had an easy pregnancy. I loved getting the nursery ready, going to my baby showers, and having an excuse to eat. My husband and I picked out a name, went to classes, and had many talks that began with, "I wonder if he…"

Near the end of my pregnancy the reality of delivery hit me. I was so wrapped up in my pregnancy that I hadn't thought about what was involved in the birth process. Fear and anticipation crept in. The day finally came for me to deliver my son—a week late!

Exhausted from a long labor, I watched as nurses took the baby to the nursery so I could rest. A knock on the door woke me. The nurse said, "We have been trying to get him to calm down, but we think he wants his mother." Groggy and still confused, I realized she was talking to me. She put my baby boy in my arms and his cries ceased instantly. At that moment, I became a mother. My life would never be the same.

After spending seven months at home with my baby, it was time for me to go back to work. God placed the most amazing woman in my path to care for my son. Miss Penny, who was a wonderful woman devoted to God, rose early and spent time with the Lord. She prayed for the children she cared for and had a wonderful peace about her. I soon realized not only was she placed in our lives to care for my son, but for me as well. She was the example of the kind of godly wife and mother I longed to be. She introduced me to the Lord in a way I had never known Him. She taught me how to pray and study His Word. She gave me wisdom, encouragement, and love.

Transformed

Prior to motherhood, painful experiences in my past had left me broken and full of anger. I didn't think about the words that came out of my mouth. I didn't think about how ugly they sounded and their effect on others. I lived a very self-centered, it's-all-about-me life. My new responsibilities as a mother suddenly propelled me into the role of protector. I wanted to shield my precious gift from all the hurts I felt as a child. I desired to live with a forgiving heart and become a kinder, gentler person. For the first time in my life, I longed to be a reflection of Christ, and an example for my son.

"If you see my smiling face, you know it is positive." I had no idea the journey God would take me on the day I walked into my husband's office, but I am forever grateful that God chose to use the birth of my son to lead me closer to His Son.

Andrea Brown (www.crosstrainersllc.com) is thankful for the gift of her children, Garrett and Savannah. They and her husband, Jimmy, her childhood sweetheart, are a constant reminder of God's blessings. She is a writer, speaker, and fitness expert, and encourages everyone to be strong from the inside out.

Madison Meenan

My Little Sister

THE SKY WAS the brightest blue I have ever seen. My entire body absorbed the sun's warmth like solar panels while I reflected on the blessings in my life. This kind of thinking always made me feel better after something stressful.

Peace and quiet were almost non-existent at home, with my younger sister constantly bragging about how amazingly she always performed at school. Being an older sister, I really hated it, especially since a decent amount of my time and effort was put into her work without getting any credit. This frustrated me immensely, and my time of relaxation ended on a short walk home from the park.

With every step my muscles tightened and my fists clenched. Cary had many little corkscrews that are not typical in your everyday obnoxious little sister. She always wore too much makeup for an eleven-year-old, along with the boyfriend she had at school, and most impressive was that she was all-around more popular than I was. Maybe it was because she played the role of actress in order to acquire attention. Her entire life was based on the emotions she had at the time.

As soon as I walked into our house, my ears were blasted by the sound of Justin Bieber singing one of my sister's favorite songs. She was dancing in the middle of our small living room like a rabid monkey.

At first I thought it was cute at least, before she started singing along with it. When Mom and Dad got home from a night of drinking, they wouldn't be happy with all the loud noise. After an hour, the music finally stopped and she went to her room to text. I went to bed as well, but my sleep didn't last long.

Around 11 p.m., my sister frantically shook me awake.

"What!" I yelled.

"Someone's trying to break into the house," she choked out with tears flooding her eyes.

We remained silent for a moment in utter terror. I heard the faint sound of two men whispering outside my window. Adrenaline started pumping through my veins. *What should I do?*

My bedroom window shattered. Glass fell like tacks all across my room. Out of sheer panic, I grabbed Cary's trembling hand and ran straight for the front door. But the second I opened it, a man's hands clasped onto Cary's and my skinny arms.

I screamed as loud as my lungs could project, and it was a deafening scream. The robber's burly arm wrapped around my mouth while he still hung onto Cary. He threw us back into the house and muttered curses.

Paralyzed and incredibly helpless, we watched the three men ravage our home, looking for anything of value. They tossed over furniture and demolished nearly everything breakable while Cary wept silently in my arms, mascara streaming down her checks. The robbers never even took a passing glance at us until they found nothing but our old television set.

"This was a waste!" said the first robber, obviously the leader of the three.

"I told you we should've hit a better neighborhood," the third robber said. "Think someone heard the girl scream?"

"The police would've been here by now," the second robber said. "But maybe we can hold 'em for ransom or just kill 'em. Your choice, boss."

I held my breath and silently prayed, thinking it would be my last few minutes on earth. *My dear Lord, thank You for all of the blessings you've given me, even my sister; only now do I realize how much I really love her, and how I can never live without her little corkscrews. God, please, give the robbers compassion to spare her and take me instead.*

I cried along with Cary and held her tighter. The leader took too long to decide what to do. I wanted it to be over with.

"No," he finally said. "We've spent too much time here already."

The men made another sweep of the house and were soon gone. I was in complete shock. Why didn't they kill us? I leaned over and kissed Cary's head over and over.

I never saw or heard of the robbers again.

From that day on, I never looked at Cary the same way again. Everything she did was beautiful, like the way she danced or sang. Things I would've missed if the robbers had taken her life. This situation of almost losing her brought me to a realization of how precious she is.

This work of fiction is by Madison Meenan, a fourteen-year-old writer from Albuquerque. She enjoys drawing, sculpting, and making terrariums. She goes to Victory Christian School and lives with her loving mom and drama queen sister, Mckenzie.

Amy Meyer Allen

Oh, the Life of a Butterfly!

SLOW MOVING, CONFINED to the earth, easy prey. This is the life of a caterpillar. Weightless wings, floating on the wind, mesmerizing beauty. Oh, the life of a butterfly!

I felt no desire to leave my comfortable life. But there I sat, alone in the cocoon built around myself. How did I get here? Dark, formidable, unwelcoming, and completely unfamiliar, I mourned for the life I once knew. The dark addictions of pornography, affairs, and prostitutes had seized my husband and stolen him away from me. With shattered dreams, a looming divorce, and 3,000 miles between us, it seemed I would never escape the betrayal that kept me locked within the boundaries of my cocoon.

For weeks it felt like a prison sentence. I lost my identity. The sorrow grew deep. No one could ease the pain.

In the dark confines of that unfamiliar place, I began to understand I wasn't alone. A supernatural presence was creating something new. I allowed the truth of God's Word to permeate my heart, bringing about change from within.

"I love you. I will never leave you or forsake you," He whispered. "I have a perfect plan for your life."

I grew to love the quiet hours I spent alone with God during my cocoon time, letting His truth transform me. Hope for a future quietly replaced my fears.

Emerging from the cocoon didn't happen overnight, as much as I would have liked it to. But God's timing is perfect and cannot be rushed.

Trials that come into my life now, I view as opportunities to be transformed. God intends the changes He creates within me to be permanent. I can't go back to being a caterpillar. Why would I want to anyway, with so many limitations, always vulnerable to predators, and a limited view of the world?

Transformed

I want to soar to new heights, see the world from a higher perspective, be released from the weight of the world. Oh, the life of a butterfly!

Amy Meyer Allen loves to write, illustrate, and design. Along with her graphic design work, she operates Humble Bumbles® and shares a marriage ministry with her husband, Tim. He and Amy live in Albuquerque, New Mexico, with their two young girls, Alila and Zoie.

Sherry L. Meneley

Feral

WHY DID I ever start feeding it?

Its name is Dupee (do-pee). That's what I call him.

As the previous homeowner handed me house keys, she pointed to a cat wandering the back yard. "Will you feed it?" she asked. "I've been giving it food and want to know it'll be taken care of."

I loved cats, had two of my own, and this woman was kind. With annoyance and a little guilt at her unexpected house-warming gift, I agreed to her request. No harm, no foul.

Over the next six months I never saw Dupee. I presumed the truth was the prior homeowners came to their senses, returned, and took their cat with them.

But then spring came. Like long forgotten bulbs in the frozen winter's ground, Dupee suddenly appeared. His face had been mangled badly. His nose, raw hamburger, and the white furred-face was caked with dirt and blood.

It was obvious, this cat would die.

But it wasn't my problem. It hadn't been around. Somehow it survived all these months. That cat was someone else's issue. I did my best to ignore it and not feel guilty.

In the evenings I sat with my beautiful Bengal cats. Their silken coats had perfect leopard rosette markings that glistened during cozy fireplace nights. The cats are lavishly loved, fed the best food, catered with $7.99 toys. Between my affection and their comfort, they wanted nothing.

During the wet cold months of spring, my mind occasionally wandered to Dupee. I didn't want to think about him. I didn't want to feel guilty. I didn't want to get involved.

As spring approached, I tried to keep an emotionally-detached watch on Dupee. His face was getting better. How he survived such an injury, fending for himself during a drenching spring that brought hail, biting winds, and a small snow flurry, was beyond me. Yet there he was in the back yard. Sitting under the pines. Healing.

One sunny post-storm afternoon, curiosity got the better of me. I set out to inspect the feral. Thinking he'd run away, I approached with caution. I stooped down and softly called, "Kitty?"

Dupee blinked back with both eyes, a cat's sign of trust. Stepping closer, Dupee got up as if to turn and dart to safety. I don't recall what I said. I just kept talking, gently, sweetly, inspecting its wounds from a distance.

After a couple of minutes, I'd seen enough and sloshed back to the house through rain-soaked grass. Turning back, I looked with pity. I was startled, he was following me! Feeling alarmed, I picked up pace; Dupee trotted then broke into a run to catch me.

My heart raced! I feared Dupee would pounce and dig its claws into my legs, scramble up my back, and scratch my eyes out. *I've read too many horror books with revengeful animals.*

Dupee caught up and swirled my legs. He purred and pawed the ground and my feet. With dissolved anxiety, I scratched his head with caution. The purring intensified and droplets of his joy-filled drool sprinkled the ground like the first signs of a spring rain.

That was the day my heart broke for this homeless cat.

That day, Dupee was fed a full meal.

That was the day this feral and I began our friendship.

Dupee returns every day. He never runs away. In fact quite the opposite has happened; he runs to me. Sometimes I think I am the only one loving this gypsy cat. In me, he found compassion in a world of uncertainty.

Dupee and my heart—are the same creatures. We've been loved and forgotten. Cared for, then left behind and homeless. Beaten and mangled and ravished by beasts. Some saw the wounds, knew the need for intervention and care, yet turned away; it wasn't their problem. It wasn't their mess.

And like Dupee, somehow, over the harshest of seasons my heart survived. It healed. It has become brave, seeks new friendships, and ventures, and places to trust again. Dupee taught me to not give up—on myself or others.

Love is a vulnerable hope, a tremendous trust and badge of courage. It transforms, cures, and restores.

Sherry L. Meneley is an author, artist, dreamer, and believer. God-sized dreams have taken her on paths helping others with spiritual healing. Through writing, art instruction at her foundation CreateHEART, and as a life coach—her desire is always to instill hope, love, and reach the unreached. www.sherrymeneley.com

Aaron Zook

Capitulation

I PERCHED ON the medical bed in Balad, Iraq, waiting for the doctor's verdict. It was Saturday morning, 18 October 2003. I sat alone. The white sheets of ten medical beds and the tan walls of the tent opened a flood of memories.

In six months, I had deployed twice to the Iraqi theater of operations. Even before the first deployment from Germany, a military doctor had called me into his office and intervened.

"You're non-deployable," he said.

"Impossible." I edged forward on my chair. "Why?"

"Your right kidney is nonfunctioning."

"But I've got to deploy. I'm a battalion commander." My hands squeezed the padded chair arms.

My wife shifted closer to me in her chair.

"Rank and position doesn't matter, in this case." The doctor slid an ultrasound picture toward me. "The large white oval is your right kidney. Just a bag of fluid. Your extreme high blood pressure and severe headaches may be caused by a blocked renal artery that feeds your working kidney."

My life of service as an Army officer screeched to a halt. Non-deployability might get me thrown out of the Army. I couldn't serve. *I'm useless.* Twenty-four years of total military service severed in an instant. I grabbed a Kleenex®, dabbed at my teary eyes and blew my nose. *God, what are you doing? Help me fight this.*

"We deploy in two months. How can I become deployable again?"

"Not sure," he replied. "We need more data."

Consultations in Germany and Walter Reed Army Medical Center in Washington, D.C. provided a quick solution—angioplasty. Walter Reed doctors ballooned out my left renal artery, but the head surgeon warned me it might only last six months. Then I would need bypass surgery.

I deployed with my battalion on schedule for Operation Iraqi Freedom. Weeks later at Camp Virginia, Kuwait, croup-like symptoms from lungs clogged by the swirling desert dust and sand storms attacked my body. My blood pressure spiked and the headaches returned. *Now what, Lord?*

I sent the first part of my battalion into Iraq, but days later, I went south in Kuwait to see a doctor. The doctor looked straight into my eyes. "I'm medevacking you. You don't belong in theater."

My shoulders slumped. Betrayed by my body—again.

I returned to Germany, then flew to Walter Reed with my wife for renal artery bypass surgery. Ten hours in the operating room. My good kidney stopped and had to be restarted, but I survived.

Three months later, after medical evaluation, I was back in Balad, Iraq, in my position as battalion commander. Our battalion accomplished major missions; however, seventy days after redeployment, here I was fidgeting on white sheets in a doctor's tan medical tent.

The doctor walked in, shaking his head. The results weren't good.

"Tell you what," the doctor picked up his clipboard, "I'll run one more blood test. If the results are worse, I'm medevacking you back home today."

That seemed reasonable. I quit fighting. "Okay." I scooted back on the bed, looking upward. *Lord, give me a sign. I know You want me here.* If I had to leave theater again, I'd be disgraced, ashamed, broken. I waited again for the results, stomach churning. I recalled Scriptures to calm down.

The doctor returned, shrugged, and shoved a paper into my hand. "You're leaving today."

I couldn't breathe.

A chopper whisked me away at seven o'clock that evening.

I wasn't kicked out of the military but had to leave command for medical reasons. My battalion successfully completed their tour in theater under another commander.

As I picked up the pieces of my life and career in my new assignment at the Pentagon, God used my wife, the Bible, and Christian friends to renew my strength. I worshiped the Lord, laying my brokenness in His healing arms. I recovered. Changed.

I re-learned to trust in God's strength and wisdom, not my own. I surrendered everything. Through His providence I went to the Army War College and celebrated another promotion, this time to Colonel.

My final assignment was to beautiful Hawaii. Two new medical issues requiring major and minor surgery didn't throw me off track. I didn't apply for higher command positions but instead served God and country at peace inside. My family, the Christian body of believers, my commander, and my soldiers supported me through these difficult circumstances. His plan was the focus, not mine. And everything worked together for His good and His glory.

Aaron M. Zook, Jr., a retired U.S. Army Colonel, enjoys writing Christian music and books. His wife and family are the joy of his life. Look for his middle-reader mystery/adventure book for boys, *The Secrets of the Castle*, published by WinePress in the summer of 2012. Check it out at www.lightwalkerministries.com.

Breaking Free

YOU CAN'T TAKE that in." I stood at the entrance to Phillips State Prison. My heart raced as the guard told me I'd have to part with my purse. Something about clutching my purse made me feel secure, but I reluctantly returned it to the car. Armed with a pink notebook and a pen, I entered the gatehouse again.

"Put those in here and walk through." The guard directed me through the metal detector. "Lift your pants," he said without emotion, sure I'd know what he was talking about.

"Huh?"

He motioned to the legs of my full-cut dress slacks.

"Oh." I lifted my trouser hems, and the thought of concealing a weapon created a nervous giggle. What was I doing here?

"I was in prison and you came to visit me."

—Matthew 25:36 NIV

I was writing a book on how to live out the call of Matthew 25, but realized I didn't know much about prison. I wasn't even sure I wanted to be there. Dressed in navy slacks, a white-collared shirt, buttoned to the top, and my wedding band, I tried not to draw attention to myself.

When I made it through the maze of locks to the inner campus, I was shocked to find men walking freely. Weren't they supposed to be cuffed and chained? They were murderers, after all. Those I passed on the way to the classroom nodded, and we eyed each other—me taking in their tattoos and they equally curious about my starched collar and Bible.

The local seminary was offering a ministry degree program inside the prison for a select group of men, and I was invited to sit in on a class. I found a spot in the classroom and perched high on my stool, waiting. Before I had time to change my mind and run, the door swung open and in marched a class of convicts. Each walked by to greet me with a handshake, and I was honestly surprised, not realizing they would be allowed to touch me. I longed for the sanitizer in my purse, which might as well have been miles away.

One man, in particular, caught my eye. I'd never seen so many tattoos up close. He shook my hand and then smiled when he caught me staring at the intricate art covering his arms. The men started class with prayer, and I was moved by their requests. They prayed not just for their families, but also for other inmates. They prayed over court dates and death row sentencing. They prayed for the loved ones of a man who was executed only days before. I blinked to make sure I wasn't in a dream.

I'd been viewing the world through stereotype lenses. Once I removed those glasses, I saw these men in a different light. Through subsequent visits, I learned Roger's daughter, Jennifer, was putting herself through nursing school. Reggie's brother was a therapist. Fredrick was grieving the death of his daughter. Without my knowledge, these felons crept inside my heart and took up residence. When my newborn daughter was in the NICU for ten days, I didn't expect a greeting card from thirty-two convicts covered with handwritten prayers. When I opened it, I wept.

Two years later, I watched with pride as each of these prisoners walked across the stage to receive their seminary degrees. Now each of them would be transferred to prisons across the state to become missionaries in dark places.

After the graduation program, I mingled with the prisoners and their families. My friend with the tattooed arms introduced me to his parents.

I bubbled with excitement, "You must be so proud of your son." Startled, she squeezed my hand, and in silence, her eyes leaked tears.

Taking my hand in both of hers she said, "No one has ever told me that."

I wrapped my arms around her and cried. He was her baby.

God has the amazing power to transform lives. But the biggest transformation wasn't with the men in the caps and gowns with prison uniforms peeking from underneath. The biggest transformation was in me. I looked around the room at my friends, and I didn't see the tattoos and gold teeth. As I looked at each of the changed lives that day, I saw each of them as somebody's baby—God's.

Carol Hatcher is a boot-wearing, coffee-drinking, sassy, southern mama who loves Jesus and isn't afraid to shout it. Ask her why she loves the Lord and be prepared to "sit a spell."

Melodie Griffin

Just Across the Pasture

FROM A DISTANCE, the monstrous rock formations at the New Mexico Ghost Ranch are staggering. The locals affectionately call them "the red and yellow cliffs." These chunky, colorful masses have been formed by years of sediment, weathering, and time. The full impact of their beauty can only be experienced from a distance—the swimming colors of red, orange, and yellow—the mingling of hues and textures. Yes, from afar, one can experience the grandeur of God's pottery wheel, the art formed from His steady, intricate, skillful brush. The red and yellow cliffs are beautiful beyond adequate description—broad, grand, perfect, logical, continuous, masterful.

But what words would describe the same view from a closer proximity? What would describe the current, the tactile? Monochrome, jagged, treacherous, grainy, gritty. The pebbles crunch underneath my feet, at times causing me to lose my footing. The dry heat parches my lips and squeezes my chest cavity like a corset. I am too close to see the dancing of colors—all my eyes can capture is a concentrated glimpse of boring beige. The smell of the cracked earth around me is not that of quenched earth after a spring rain, but of dusty sand and rock that have sat thirsty. The dust makes me cough. Is this the same creation others who sit across the pasture can see?

The often-quoted Romans 8:28 remains in effect. Somehow, someway, God "takes all things and works them together for our good." Using time as His carving knife, He gradually transforms each layer into something marvelous—something complimentary to the whole. When my nose is pressed firmly against the dust of my current hardship, my focus is skewed. I only see the jagged edges of difficulty and forget there is a much bigger story being written. To see the better, bigger view, I must go across the pasture. I must be intentional about finding my Sabbath to hear the voice of the Author. I must afford Him the opportunity to change my perspective.

Just Across the Pasture

When I am drowning in the unforeseen sea of heartache, I am convinced this season will last forever. There is no rescue. God transfigures my perspective to remind me this is temporary. He is doing something bigger than my eyes can see. Something immaculate. When I am gleefully splashing around in the fountains of happy times, God gently reminds me that this, too, is only a season, and hard times will come again. While not the most pleasant of thoughts, a transformed perspective remembers the same God who brought me out of the last trial will also bring me through the next time of sorrow. He is faithful. He redeems.

So on this treacherous, imperfect journey of life, I will choose to seek God's perspective from just across the pasture. For it is there that I see the grandeur of the masterpiece. It is there my lungs can fill fully with the oxygen of God's sovereignty. And after the transformation of perspective, it is there I am refueled to tie my hiking boots and make my way across the pasture to the red and yellow cliffs of life.

Melodie Griffin is an inspirational speaker, recording artist, and freelance writer. She is a member of the CLASS faculty and does laundry in her spare time. South Carolina is home to Melodie, her husband, their three children, and two Westie dogs. Catch up with her at www. melodiegriffin.com and www.speakerchicks.com.

Tama Westman

Earth to Tama

LOST. EMOTIONALLY, PHYSICALLY, spiritually, relationally. Oh, yes, I have been lost. So lost, I courted drastic measures to revive some sense of feeling, purpose, or passion.

Is it possible to drift through life without a rudder to guide, even when all is well, food's in the fridge, money's in the bank, and the family is floating on an even keel?

Yes.

Our culture places a high priority on balance. We expend an inordinate amount of energy on being "happy."

However, the writer's life can be lonesome, disparate. We wrap ourselves into the thoughts we press to page, often forgetting to connect with God, friends, and family. But this creates a void in our lives, a place where unhappiness thrives. After all, we were created specifically as relational creatures.

I was lost. Dark. Depressed. Done. There was nothing externally wrong. No disaster loomed. Yet, I felt empty, without direction, guided by a map without a key.

My life as a writer was over. I was sure of it. No stories lurked in the brain waiting to be written. Rather than writing, I played "Angry Birds," planted a garden, and found innumerable hours to throw the Frisbee® to Oreo, my border collie.

I embraced the darkness. And though I grew somber for several months, and lost valuable time where I might have written a book, still, I sensed a stretching deep inside. Great lessons can be found when one delves into the darkness, searching for deeper feeling, clearer purpose, and renewed passion. By learning to linger where God takes me, even in those darker recesses of my soul, I have unearthed layers of emotion, love, and understanding I never experienced before.

Pleased with this new growth, I was content—or so I told myself—to let the writing go. I purged files, canceled contracts, and withdrew from everything, and everyone, connected to my writing life. I focused on my daughter, my son, cooking, cleaning, being depressed, yes, and "Angry Birds."

I grew to love the darkness. There, no one expected anything of me. I was free from responsibility, absent of care. Void of emotion, I waited. I guess that's really the heart of my hiatus, waiting.

I waited to see what my new chapter would be. Was I freeing myself to become a doting grandmother? Had I detangled so I could re-enter the workforce? Would I travel? Disappear?

Ooh. Had that thought actually crossed my mind? Though I'd learned to wait, to listen, even to tiptoe through others lives where before I'd stomped, still if you reside in the darkness too long, you can lose track of the path back to light.

A change in scenery, that's what I needed. I packed the car, and headed to a cabin on the North Shore. Several days in, the campground manager delivered a message that my husband had called.

I dragged out my cell phone, and drove a few miles until I found service. Pulling to the side of the road, I dialed his number.

"Hey, did you need something?" I asked.

"I need you. Are you coming home?"

He knew. He hadn't asked *when* are you coming home, but *whether*.

"I..." I couldn't finish the sentence. So lost within myself, words were no longer my friends. I had none to give.

"Honey, I don't know what you're going through, but I believe God's got something great for you. Ask Him to reveal it to you now. Then come home."

That was it! I needed to be needed. The light snapped back on inside. I asked God if I was washed up, or if He might be able to use me yet.

He woke me in the middle of the night with His answers. With an idea so thrilling, so fascinating, I couldn't go back to sleep. I cranked up the computer, ignored the "Angry Birds" icon, and began to write. Fiction!

Are you sure, Lord? I'm not a fiction writer.

"You are who I need you to be," I heard. Transformed.

Following His lead, I became passionate about what He gave me to create, thrilled with the conversations He and I have in the dark hours before dawn.

My relationships are deeper as I now meet others where they are, rather than attempting to drag them to where I am. My husband's always said it takes "you, me, and He" (inaccurate as his grammar may be) for life to work. Remembering that, I'm no longer lost; I'm home.

Transformed

Henry David Thoreau said, "Not until we are lost do we begin to understand ourselves." My dark interlude gave me a greater understanding of others, and of myself. Taking God's hand, I write on.

Tama Westman has written over 1000 articles and has stories included in several compilations, including *Along the Way for Teens* and the *Groovy Chicks' Road Trip to Love*. Currently she is working on the first of three novels in a series, though her apologies to Oreo are constant.

Changed

Karen Porter

AS A CHILD, I often went to my grandmother's country home. I was free to roam the fields, pastures, and woods nearby, no longer hemmed in by the fears found in city streets. What freedom! Walking in the fields, I could be anything. And I tried it all. I danced like a ballerina, twirled my baton like a pro, and promenaded like a princess. What potential! I sang to the top of my voice and even preached a few sermons to the cattle. What ability! At the edge of the woods, my brother built a play town complete with roads and bridges. In that make-believe world, I was the president. What power!

When I became a Christian, I experienced some of those same emotions on a deeper level. Those early feelings of potential, ability, and power became real because I was a new creature who had God at my side. Paul said, "*Therefore, if anyone is in Christ, he is a new creation; the old has gone, the new has come!*" (2 Corinthians 5:17-18 NIV).

What does it mean to be a new creature? In Romans 12:2, Paul instructed us to be transformed. The word transformed is translated from the Greek word *metamorphoo*. Do you remember the English word metamorphosis from seventh grade biology? Metamorphosis is change. God longs to change us into new creatures. A look into the animal kingdom will help us understand God's desire for us.

In those same fields at my grandmother's house, there were thousands of grasshoppers. As I walked through the tall grass, they led the way hopping out of my path. There were large ones and small ones, brown, white, and green. At first, I assumed the small ones were babies and the large ones adults, but there was no way to tell. The tiniest creature may have been the oldest adult. They all looked the same.

Some of us are like the grasshopper. We are older but we are not much different than when we were novice believers. We are leaders yet we display childish attributes: envy, selfishness, and pride. These attitudes are disguised as concern for the purity of the church or doctrinal positions.

They show up in business meeting arguments or whispered complaints about the pastor, the music, or the programs. We have grown up but we have not grown.

The tadpole changes more than the grasshopper. He is born with gills and fins and swims. When he is transformed, he loses the tail and develops lungs and strong legs. He begins to hop out of the water and breathes air. Once quiet, he now has a bullfrog voice. Once water bound, he is now free. The frog is completely changed in appearance and actions, but continues to live around the pond. He sits on the lily pads and occasionally jumps into the water for a swim.

Some of us have also made huge changes, but like the frog we still cling to the old life. The old language, old parties, and old desires are gone. But we sometimes dabble in our old ways, watching the same TV programs, reading the same books, and going to the same places. There is no freedom in a dual life.

Truly transformed Christians are like the caterpillar that enters the chrysalis and emerges as a colorful butterfly able to fly free. No longer a brown worm inching its way along the ground, the butterfly experiences all the beauty and freedom of flight.

God intends for us to fly free. Like the butterfly. We should defy gravity and soar. God longs to see us reach heights we have never experienced before. In fact, his greatest desire for us is that we will become like Him. As Paul told the believers at Corinth, we can be transformed and changed into the likeness of Christ.

Being like Christ means freedom, potential, and power.

Karen Porter is an international retreat and seminar speaker, author of six books, and a successful businesswoman. She flies free near Houston, Texas. Learn more about Karen at www.karenporter. com and her communication consulting business at www.kaecreativesolutions.com.

About CLASSEMINARS, Inc.

CLASSEMINARS is America's premier trainer of Christian speakers, writers, and leaders.

CLASSEMINARS provides courses of all types to help Christian communicators speak with power and write with passion.

In addition to developing speaking skills and helping authors onto the publishing road, CLASS offers training and certification in the field of The Personalities for personal and professional use. CLASS Career Coaching programs assist writers and speakers in building careers, ministries, and platforms.

More than 30,000 men and women have been influenced by the powerful preparation and guidance of CLASSEMINARS.

Attend a CLASS event coming soon to a city near you.
For more information go to our website at www.classeminars.org

CPSIA information can be obtained at www.ICGtesting.com
Printed in the USA
LVOW130811211211

260374LV00002B/8/P